T

John Milton's

Paradise Lost

Text by
Corinna Siebert Ruth
(M.A., California State University-Fresno)
Department of English
Fresno Pacific College
Fresno, California

Illustrations by
Karen Pica

R**E**A Res⋯ ⋯ion Association

MAXnotes™ for
PARADISE LOST

Copyright © 1995 by Research & Education
Association. All rights reserved. No part of this
book may be reproduced in any form without
permission of the publisher.

Printed in the United States of America

Library of Congress Catalog Card Number 95-67777

International Standard Book Number 0-87891-992-9

MAXnotes™ is a trademark of
Research & Education Association, Piscataway, New Jersey 08854

I-1

What **MAXnotes**™ *Will Do for You*

This book is intended to help you absorb the essential contents and features of John Milton's *Paradise Lost* and to help you gain a thorough understanding of the work. The book has been designed to do this more quickly and effectively than any other study guide.

For best results, this **MAXnotes** book should be used as a companion to the actual work, not instead of it. The interaction between the two will greatly benefit you.

To help you in your studies, this book presents the most up-to-date interpretations of every section of the actual work, followed by questions and fully explained answers that will enable you to analyze the material critically. The questions also will help you to test your understanding of the work and will prepare you for discussions and exams.

Meaningful illustrations are included to further enhance your understanding and enjoyment of the literary work. The illustrations are designed to place you into the mood and spirit of the work's settings.

The **MAXnotes** also include summaries, character lists, explanations of plot, and chapter-by-chapter analyses. A biography of the author and discussion of the work's historical context will help you put this literary piece into the proper perspective of what is taking place.

The use of this study guide will save you the hours of preparation time that would ordinarily be required to arrive at a complete grasp of this work of literature. You will be well prepared for classroom discussions, homework, and exams. The guidelines that are included for writing papers and reports on various topics will prepare you for any added work which may be assigned.

The **MAXnotes** will take your grades "to the max."

Dr. Max Fogiel
Program Director

Contents

Section One: *Introduction* 1
  The Life and Work of John Milton 1
  Historical Background 3
  Master List of Characters 5
  Summary of the Work 7
  Estimated Reading Time 9

> **Each book includes List of Characters,**
> **Summary, Analysis, Study Questions and**
> **Answers, and Suggested Essay Topics.**

Section Two: *Paradise Lost* 10
  Book I 10
  Book II 20

Book III 30

Book IV... 40

Book V 50

Book VI 60

Book VII 71

Book VIII 79

Book IX... 87

Book X 102

Book XI... 111

Book XII 120

Section Three: *Sample Analytical Paper Topics* 129

Section Four: *Bibliography*...................................... 135

Introduction

The Life and Work of John Milton

John Milton left a rich legacy of English poetry and prose comprised of sonnets, lyric and epic poems, and controversial political and social pamphlets defending divorce, freedom of the press, and the Puritan cause. He was born in London on December 9, 1608. Though his father had been disinherited for transferring his allegiance from the Catholic to the Protestant church, he had made a substantial fortune as a scrivener and had also dabbled in money lending. As a talented musician, perhaps a professional, Milton's father would have kept company with artists and patrons alike. From early childhood the young Milton was exposed to the culturally rich atmosphere of seventeenth-century London. It is noteworthy that Shakespeare was still writing plays when Milton was born.

Recognizing their son's exceptional intellectual aptitude, his parents provided private tutors for him at an early age. In 1620, he attended St. Paul's school in London with Alexander Gill as his tutor. When he was 17, Milton entered Christ's College at Cambridge. His first years at Cambridge were not as happy as they had been at St. Paul's. Milton left college in his second year after a quarrel with his tutor, William Chappel. When he returned, he was assigned to a more compatible tutor, Nathaniel Tovey. Milton took his B. A. degree from Cambridge in 1629 and his M. A. three years later.

Though it had been Milton's intention to become a clergyman, his disillusionment with the Church of England under the leadership of Archbishop Laud had led him to direct his course toward the writing of poetry instead. Following his years at Cambridge, he went to live with his parents at Horton, their newly acquired country estate, where he enjoyed a period of "uninterrupted leisure." Here he devoted his time to writing poetry and studying the Greek and Latin authors.

After the death of Milton's mother, his younger brother, Christopher, moved to Horton with his new wife. Perhaps his broken solitude and the loss of his mother influenced Milton to leave the family home and travel to the European continent in 1638. His travels through France and Italy, where he met many distinguished intellectuals and literary men, proved to be 16 of the most rewarding months of his life.

Upon arrival in England in 1639, Milton established residency in London. His nine-year-old nephew, John Phillips, boarded with him, receiving private tutoring. A year later John's older brother, Edward, joined them. When several other boarders moved in for private lessons, Milton's house began to resemble a small, private boarding school.

In 1642, Milton began to compose the dramatic version of *Paradise Lost* based on the ancient Greek model of tragedy. That same year, Milton, now 35 years old, brought a 17-year-old bride, Mary Powell, into the scholarly atmosphere of his boarding school. Her aversion to the studious life, along with the differences in their ages and interests, resulted in an unfortunate match. After several months she went back to her parents for a visit and did not return. The Powells, a strong Royalist family, were perhaps afraid of their daughter's close association with Milton, a parliamentarian who had openly opposed the King's cause. Milton's rebuttal to his wife's desertion took the form of a series of pamphlets defending divorce on the grounds of incompatibility. Mary Powell returned to him after two years of separation. The Royalist cause had been defeated, and the Powell family needed Milton's protection. His wife and several of her family members moved in with him, resulting in noise and confusion that was not conducive to scholarly concentration.

Mary Powell bore him four children. In 1652, Milton's fortunes rapidly declined when his only son died. It was in the same year that Milton became totally blind. The following year his wife died just after the birth of his third daughter. At the age of 45, Milton, in his desolation, was a blind widower with three small children, Anne, six years old, Mary, only three, and Deborah, an infant.

After five years he married Katharine Woodcock, but the happy marriage ended when she, along with their three-month-old son, died 16 months later. In 1663, he married Elizabeth Minshull, a 24-year-old woman who gave him the support and stability that had been lacking with his three grown daughters. He had sought their help as readers and amanuenses in his work, but they had, without his knowledge, attempted to sell his books and other possessions.

Milton died on November 8, 1674, from a sudden attack of gout or rheumatism. He was buried in St. Giles Cripplegate near his father. Elizabeth Minshull lived to cherish his memory, providing biographers with valuable information about his final years.

Historical Background

Milton's writings were heavily influenced by the political and religious climate of his day. When Charles I became king in 1625, he repeatedly dissolved the Parliament whenever the members would not defer to his wishes. In his eagerness for complete power, King Charles finally ruled without Parliament altogether for 11 years. The King promoted William Laud to Archbishop of Canterbury in 1633. Laud became omnipotent in both church and state. He used his authority to impose certain religious ceremonies in the Church of England and forced the use of the prayer book on the populace. In preparing a list of the clergy for King Charles, Laud labelled each name with an O for orthodox or P for Puritan. The Puritans were identified for suppression, while the orthodox were designated as possible candidates for promotion. He went as far as ordering the justices of the peace to search houses and bring people before the commissions if they were caught holding private religious services. It became increasingly difficult for Milton to consider committing himself to a career as a minister of the church under the tyranny of Archbishop Laud.

Civil war finally broke out and Charles I was beheaded by the Puritans. Milton responded with a series of pamphlets in support of regicide. He defended the deposition and execution of the King in *The Tenure of Kings and Magistrates,* and argued against the power of the bishops in *Of Reformation in England.* These publications brought him an appointment as Latin Secretary under Oliver Cromwell's Commonwealth government.

At the time of the Restoration, when King Charles II replaced the Commonwealth, Milton went into hiding for a time. He was finally taken into custody but released for a substantial fee. There has been much discussion concerning the reasons for Milton's release. Many men who were guilty of fewer political crimes than Milton were put to death. It is believed that Andrew Marvell, the poet, was one of his friends in the council who interceded for him.

Though Milton's pamphlets, written in his middle years, reflect the political and religious life of seventeenth century England, his poetry depicts the cultural aspects of those times. "L' Allegro" and "Il Penseroso" are companion poems written in his early years. During his days at Horton he wrote "Comus," a masque with music by Henry Lawes, and "Lycidas," a pastoral elegy. Though he had sketched his idea in dramatic form as early as 1642, it was not until he had given up his post as Latin Secretary and become totally blind that he began work on the epic poem *Paradise Lost*. Published in 1667, it was followed by *Paradise Regained* and *Samson Agonistes*, both published in 1671.

Paradise Lost, written in blank verse, follows the common characteristics of the epic that were established by Homer. The epic is a long, narrative poem, written in an exalted tone and an elevated style, glorifying characters of high position. The epic hero is a noble character with heroic stature whose virtues represent a particular culture or race and are of great historical or legendary significance. The setting is vast, covering a whole nation or the entire universe. The action consists of deeds of courage and boldness. Supernatural beings—gods, angels, and demons—periodically intervene in the action.

To these characteristics are added some common conventions or devices employed by the poet who begins by stating his theme and invoking the muse or some higher power to guide or inspire him. The poem opens in *medias res*—in the middle of things. The rest of the narrative, the beginning and ending, is then completed, when necessary, throughout the poem. The main characters are given long formal speeches. The expanded epic simile is employed with repeated frequency, and epic battles are described to present the conflict.

It was Milton's ambition to emulate the ancients, "Homer in Greek" and "Virgil in Latin." In the preface to *Paradise Lost*, "the measure is," Milton says, "English heroic verse without rhyme." Though he owed his medium of expression to the classical poets, Milton borrowed his subject, the "Fall of Man," from the biblical narrative in Genesis and the "War in Heaven" from Revelation. He was influenced by the Spenserian tradition of religious poetry and patterned his verse after the unrhymed iambic pentameter of Shakespeare's poetic drama.

In 1674, Andrew Marvell wrote a poem as a preface to the second edition of *Paradise Lost* in which he praised Milton whose poetry sings "with so much gravity and ease." Dryden, Milton's contemporary, was a poet who declared that Satan was Milton's "hero" in the epic poem. This idea surfaced again in the late eighteenth century when William Blake also wrote that Milton was a true poet, but was, unknown to himself, in sympathy with the rebellious Satan. But C. S. Lewis, a modern critic, refuted his idea on the grounds that it is the reader, not Milton, who admires Satan. Samuel Johnson criticized Milton's "unskillful allegory" of Sin and Death, but praised him for his composition of a great individualistic work.

By the nineteenth century, Milton had taken his place with Shakespeare, Homer, and Virgil. Matthew Arnold saw him as a master, in English, of the great epic style of the ancients. In our own century, Milton was attacked by T. S. Eliot as a poet whose visual imagery contained an inherent weakness. In comparing God to the classical Zeus, who is not a loving god, and Satan to Prometheus, who is a friend to man, Werblowsky suggests that Milton, unknowingly, transposed his main characters, leading the reader to empathize with Satan and to fear God. Stanley Fish argues, however, that it was Milton's intention to lead the reader through the Fall in order to experience the fallen state with Adam. If the reader then finds Satan attractive and God distant and unloving, he is, just as Adam was, still separated from God by his own sin.

Master List of Characters

God—*He is the omniscient creator of Heaven and Earth and all its creatures.*

The Son—*He is called "the Son" in Heaven. He has not yet come down to earth as Jesus Christ. He volunteers to give his life as a ransom for Man's sin.*

Adam—*The first man created by God and placed in the Garden of Eden, he is forbidden to eat the fruit of the Tree of Knowledge.*

Eve—*The first woman created by God from Adam's rib; like Adam, she is forbidden to eat the fruit of the Tree of Knowledge but is tempted by the Serpent and finally succumbs. She then convinces Adam to eat the fruit.*

Satan—*The archangel, Lucifer, who is cast out of Heaven for leading a group of angels in a revolt against God; he is the ruler of Hell after his fall. Disguised as the Serpent, he seduces Eve to eat the fruit from the Tree of Knowledge.*

Mulciber—*He is the architect for Pandemonium, Satan's capitol in Hell.*

Beelzebub—*A fallen angel who is the second in command in Hell; he speaks last at the "devilish council," convincing the fallen angels to accept Satan's scheme of revenge toward God, which involves the destruction of God's last creation, Man.*

Moloch—*He proposes that he and all the other fallen angels in Hell fight an "open war" with Heaven in order to reverse their miserable state.*

Belial—*A fallen angel who argues that it is better to exist in Hell than not to exist at all; he reasons that if they anger God, he might destroy them completely.*

Mammon—*He suggests to Satan's council that the fallen angels dismiss all thoughts of war against Heaven and retain their freedom in Hell. He digs for gems and gold so that Hell will equal Heaven in magnificence.*

Sin—*Satan's daughter who was born full-grown from his head; Sin was once alluring to the angels in Heaven but is now repulsive and ugly as she guards the gates of Hell with her son, Death.*

Death—*Born from the union of Satan and his daughter, Sin; Death, in turn, rapes Sin, producing "yelling monsters," the fruits of the second incestuous act.*

Chaos—*Personifies confusion and disorder in the place of "utter darkness" where he reigns with his consort, Night.*

Uriel—*An archangel who is nearest to God's throne, he is ready to serve at his command. Satan, disguised as a Cherub, deceives Uriel on his way to Earth.*

Gabriel—*God's angel, Gabriel guards Adam and Eve at the gate to Paradise.*

Abdiel—*An angel who defies Satan in the war in Heaven; Abdiel stays faithful to God.*

Michael—*Leads God's angels in battle in the war in Heaven. He instructs Adam after the fall and leads Adam and Eve out of Paradise at the end of the poem.*

Raphael—*A six-winged angel, Raphael has been sent by God from Heaven to protect Adam and Eve, warning them of the evil (Satan) that lurks in the Garden.*

Urania—*The classical muse, the Muse of Astronomy, adopted by the Christian poets for divine inspiration. Milton identifies Urania as "heavenly born."*

Summary of the Work

A short summary, entitled "The Argument," is presented by Milton as a preface to each of the 12 books of *Paradise Lost*. In the first book, he announces the subject of the poem, "Man's disobedience and the loss thereupon of Paradise." The poem opens in the "midst of things," after the war in Heaven but before the fall of Adam and Eve. Satan and his multitude of angels have been cast out of Heaven and into the "Deep" for rebelling against God and are chained on the burning lake in Hell. Satan awakens his legions of angels, comforting them in their dejected state by offering them hope of reclaiming Heaven. He recounts an old prophecy he has heard, while still in Heaven, of another world that will be created with a new kind of creature called Man. Satan calls a council in his newly erected palace, Pandemonium, to decide whether to wage another war on Heaven. After a lengthy debate, the council finally decides to send Satan to search for God's new creation instead. He flies toward the gates of Hell which are guarded by Sin and Death. They open the gates and Satan meets Chaos who directs him to the new world.

Seeing Satan flying toward Earth, God points him out to the Son, prophesying that Satan will tempt Man to sin. God demonstrates his justice by declaring his divine grace to Man, however, only if someone will offer himself as a ransom for his sin. The Son volunteers and is praised by the angels in Heaven. Meanwhile, Satan has travelled through the Limbo of Vanity and reached the orb of the sun. He quickly disguises himself as a Cherub before he asks Uriel for directions to Earth.

On Earth, Satan disguises himself as a water bird in the Tree of Life where he overlooks the beauty of Adam and Eve in their blissful state. Later that night, Satan is caught at Eve's ear, tempting her in a dream, and he flies from the Garden. In the morning, Eve relates her disturbing dream to Adam.

Raphael is sent by God to caution Adam about the evil that is lurking in Paradise. After dining, Raphael engages Adam in a long conversation, reminding him of his obedience to God though he has been given free choice. Raphael informs Adam of the war in Heaven and the victory of the Son who drove Satan and his legions over the wall of Heaven and into the Deep. The Son was later sent by God "to perform the work of creation in six days." Taking his leave, Raphael again cautions Adam to beware of God's command.

Returning to Paradise by night, Satan enters the body of the sleeping serpent. The next day, Eve innocently suggests to Adam that they work in separate areas of the Garden. Remembering Raphael's warning, Adam refuses at first but finally consents. Left alone, Eve is approached and flattered by the Serpent. He tells her his human speech and understanding were brought about by tasting of the fruit of the Tree of Knowledge. He slowly convinces Eve to eat this same fruit. Although pleased with the taste and the exhilarating feeling, Eve approaches Adam with some reluctance. She convinces him to taste the fruit, and the effects are quickly felt, prompting them to cover their nakedness and blame each other for the sinful deed.

The guardian angels ascend to Heaven, and the Son is sent to judge the sinful pair. Out of pity, he also clothes them. In anticipation of their future appearance on Earth, Sin and Death build a broad highway over Chaos to make Earth more accessible. Satan returns to Pandemonium where he is greeted with a hiss from the fallen angels now transformed into serpents.

On Earth, Adam and Eve lament their fallen state. To avoid the curse that they have brought upon future generations, Eve considers taking her life, but Adam gives her hope that the promised Messiah, their seed, will avenge Satan by overcoming Death. The Son intercedes for the earthly pair, presenting their prayers of repentance to God who forgives them but proclaims that they must leave Paradise. Michael is sent from Heaven to deliver the unhappy message. Grieving his loss of Paradise, Adam pleads with Michael but finally abides by God's orders. Michael leads Adam to a high hill where he engages in a lengthy prophecy of the future of all mankind. He explains the "incarnation, death, resurrection, and ascension" of the Son of God. Comforted by God's promise, Adam awakens Eve who has been dreaming "gentle dreams" that have composed her spirit. Taking each of them by the hand, Michael leads them out of Paradise, guarded by the Cherubim and ushered by God's blazing sword.

Estimated Reading Time

Milton's epic poetry is laced with classical and biblical allusions, and his language is elevated with a distinct departure from common speech. For an adequate understanding of the poem, it is, therefore, necessary to pay special attention to the difficult words and phrases and the allusions that are translated at the bottom of most texts of *Paradise Lost*. During the first reading, the 12 book, 282-page epic poem should be read for an understanding of the plot only. In this case, it can be read in approximately seven hours. After the initial reading, the poem should be read more carefully, making repeated use of a good dictionary and the glossary of the text to clarify the archaic language and Latinisms that frequently appear in Milton's verse. The second reading would probably take a little more than 12 hours for the entire epic poem, allowing about an hour for each book. Since the books vary from 15 to 34 pages, the reading time will not be the same for each book.

(Note: Throughout this MAXnotes volume, parenthetical source references to *Paradise Lost* are preceded by the abbreviation "P.L.")

Paradise Lost

Book I

New Characters:

Satan: *the archangel, Lucifer, cast out of Heaven and ruling in Hell*

Beelzebub: *a fallen angel, second to Satan in power*

Moloch: *a fallen angel who later proposes "open war" with Heaven*

Chemos: *a demon who was later the god of the Moabites*

Astarte: *goddess of the moon fallen from Heaven and now in Hell*

Thammuz: *a fallen angel who later became a Babylonian god, symbol of fertility*

Dagon: *a fallen angel who later became a god of the Philistines; a sea monster who is half man, half fish*

Rimmon: *a fallen angel; later became a Syrian god*

Osiris: *an Egyptian male deity*

Isis: *wife of Osiris*

Orus: *son of Osiris and Isis*

Belial: *a lewd, depraved, fallen angel who is filled with lust*

Mammon: *a fallen angel interested in finding gold in Hell*

Mulciber: *a fallen angel; architect for Pandemonium*

Summary

Milton prefaces "The Argument" to Book I of his epic poem with a defense of its unrhymed heroic verse. He declares that, besides "Homer in Greek" and "Virgil in Latin," the best English poets of tragedy have also rejected rhyme. After a brief summary of Book I, the author introduces the subject of *Paradise Lost* which is "Man's first disobedience" and his loss of Paradise. He invokes the "Heavenly Muse" or, in other words, the Holy Spirit who inspired "that shepherd," Moses, on Mt. Sinai. Insisting that his theme will be elevated above that of the pagan poets, Milton proposes to "justify the ways of God to men." He reiterates the familiar story of the fall of Adam and Eve with a reminder that it was the "infernal Serpent" who was the cause. Declaring himself as God's equal, Satan's pride and rebellion have been the reason for his expulsion from Heaven. It was the envy of God's new creation, Man, that prompted Satan's revenge when he deceived Eve and, consequently, brought sin into the world.

The first action of the poem begins with Satan, a former archangel, chained on the burning lake in Hell after he and his angels have been cast out of Heaven. It is a wild, dismal wasteland in flames with darkness all around. Satan addresses Beelzebub, who is lying next to him, and assures him that "all is not lost." He is startled by the frightening changes in Beelzebub's appearance since his fall. Satan swears that he will never repent and bow to God, but will wage "eternal war" against him. His apparent confidence, however, is "racked with deep despair." Convinced of God's strength and supremacy, Beelzebub questions Satan's optimism in this place of eternal punishment. But Satan quickly replies that they must stay strong and find ways to avenge God by changing good into evil whenever possible.

Since Heaven has given Satan free will, he recovers his strength and, followed by Beelzebub, lifts himself from the burning lake, flying to dry land. Satan concedes that here he must bid farewell to his former happy state and welcome the horrors of the "infernal world," but at least he will be free. He relishes the idea that God will be far from this place and decides that it is "Better to reign in Hell than serve in Heaven." Meanwhile, the other fallen angels still lie prostrate on the burning lake. Satan calls them to action, loudly shouting their heavenly titles, "Princes, Potentates, Warriors." At the sound of their general's voice, they spring up and take flight, filling the air like a "cloud/ Of locusts."

The poet enumerates the primary fallen angels. First is Moloch, who became the "horrid king" in biblical times, forcing children to pass through fire as human sacrifices. The list continues with Chemos, god of the Moabites, who is much like Moloch. Astarte, Thammuz, Dagon, Rimmon, Osiris, Isis, and Orus are also fallen angels who later become pagan gods and goddesses after wandering around on Earth. Belial, whose name means "wickedness," bears the distinction of depravity and lust.

With his customary pride, Satan speaks to the dejected group of angels, trying to boost their courage and dispel their fears. Azazel, the standard bearer, raises the flag as a universal shout rings out, and Satan's angels await his command. Satan attempts to speak three times but is choked with tears when he observes the "withered glory" of his loyal followers in their fallen state. He finally speaks, advocating war either against God or against his new creation, Man. The legions of angels react joyously, throwing flaming swords into the air and "hurling defiance" toward God.

Mammon leads the fallen angels to a hill to dig for gold, attempting to prove that Hell, like Heaven, has its riches. Suddenly, they encounter a temple, Pandemonium, rising like a vapor out of the hill. Built by the architect, Mulciber, it serves as Satan's capitol in Hell where he summons them to a council to decide their fate. Swarming as thick as "bees/ In springtime," they enter the capitol where they begin the consultation in an attempt to resolve the issue of war against God for the "recovery of Heaven."

Analysis

A perceptive interpretation of *Paradise Lost* must necessarily include an understanding of the epic devices employed by Milton. In imitation of Homer and Virgil, he opens the poem in "medias res"—in the midst of things. The war in Heaven has ended with the defeat of Satan and his angels who have fallen into the abyss. In keeping with the epic tradition, the poet will later return to the rebellion of Satan and the consequent battle that started the chain of events.

Milton also follows the age-old epic device of invoking the Muse to inspire him and, thereby, lend authority to his expansive theme of justifying "the ways of God to men." He calls on the Muse who had revealed the secrets of the creation story in Genesis to Moses. In the opening lines of Book VII, however, the poet invokes the muse, Urania, who was the classical muse of astronomy. The poet makes it clear that it is "the meaning, not the name" that he is calling forth. In this way he upholds the tradition of the epic, identifying himself with all the great poets of antiquity. His Muse is not one of the nine who dwelt on Mt. Olympus, but is "heavenly born." Milton is alluding to the Holy Spirit, the Muse of Moses and the prophets, who inspired the Scriptures.

In adhering to the epic convention, Milton depicts the vast settings of Heaven, Earth, and Hell. The poem also includes the regions of Chaos that Satan later travels through on his way to Earth. The distance from Hell to Heaven is, the poet says, "from the center thrice to the utmost pole." The setting of the poem stretches throughout the universe.

In the introductory lines of Book I, Milton exemplifies the grand style and exalted tone traditional to the epic, declaring to the Muse that he will pursue "things unattempted yet in prose or rhyme." With elevated language, thickly plaited with biblical, classical, and geographical allusions, the poet will attempt to glorify and justify the ways of God.

Milton frequently makes use of the device of the expanded epic simile. Satan's angels are described in a series of superb Homeric similes. "His legions, angel forms, who lay entranced/ Thick as autumnal leaves that strew the brooks." Later the angels are referred to as "a pitchy cloud/ Of locusts . . . that hung like night and darkened all the land of Nile." When Satan waves at them to direct their course, they land on the brimstone and fill the plain. "A multitude, like which the populous North/ Poured never from her frozen loins." The simile alludes to the invasions by the Roman Empire. Each of these three examples is extended to a length of approximately eight to 14 lines. Another illustration of the epic convention is seen in Milton's enumeration of Satan's fallen angels from Moloch to Belial which resembles the epic catalogue in the extended list of ships in Homer's *Iliad*.

An epic device common to the poem is the utterance of the long formal speeches by the main characters. In Book I, Satan, lying prostrate on the burning lake, addresses Beelzebub who is lying next to him. Satan renders a long, unrelenting speech, swearing to avenge God's actions. Beelzebub answers him in a speech equally as lengthy, mourning his loss of Heaven.

Milton's characterization of Satan has been the subject of much controversy among the critics. The debate has centered around the portrayal of Satan as an attractive figure who rebels against God in his personal ambition for independence. With determination, Satan demonstrates his "courage never to submit or yield," though he has been hurled by God from the "plains of Heaven." Satan is admittedly a well-drawn character whose grandiose aspirations involve his own pride. Milton's appealing delineation of Satan's character, some commentators say, forces the reader to sympathize and identify with the fallen archangel just as Milton himself does. C. S. Lewis argues, however, that although "Milton has put much of himself into Satan, it is unwarrantable to conclude that he was pleased with that part of himself or expected us to be pleased." When Satan rises to address his fallen angels in Book I, his attractiveness is still apparent since "his form had not yet lost/ All her original brightness." But throughout the poem, he is seen in a steady degeneration from an archangel who still possesses some of the qualities of his former state in Heaven, to a completely depraved creature after the fall of Man. Milton also evokes our sympathy for Satan in Book I when he depicts him weeping for his angels whose glory has withered since their fall from Heaven. When he finally speaks, he is unable to offer much hope. The more he speaks, the more he appears to be damning himself.

Satan's denial that God created him, allows him to consider himself as an equal to the Almighty. In speaking to Beelzebub on the lake of fire, Satan refuses to deify God's power since he has so recently "doubted his empire." Satan, while still in Heaven, confirms this heretical belief in Book VI when he tries to convince Abdiel to join him in rebellion against God. Abdiel tells Satan that God "made all things, even thee," but Satan challenges him.

> Remember'st thou
> Thy making, while the Maker gave thee being?
> We know no time when we were not as now;
> Know none before us, self-begot, self-raised
> By our own quickening power.
>
> P.L., Book VI, ll. 857–61

Satan's greatest sin is his refusal to see himself as God's subordinate.

Milton's consciousness of the natural order, based on the hierarchy of all beings and things, had its beginnings with Aristotle and influenced the ethics of Medieval thought. The idea still permeated the plays of Shakespeare in the late sixteenth and early seventeenth centuries and would have been readily understood by the people of Milton's day. In this hierarchy, God was supreme and all other beings, including the angels, had a superior to whom they owed obedience and an inferior whom they ruled. It extended from God to the lowest animals and even to inanimate objects. When the hierarchy was destroyed, disorder and chaos reigned. Satan's refusal to recognize his particular place in the hierarchy results in his disobedience to God and the consequent destruction of the natural harmony. Milton's seventeenth-century readers would have thought it ludicrous for Satan to think that he could rule as an equal to God and his Son in Heaven.

The abundance of biblical allusions lends credence to *Paradise Lost* as a reflection of the authoritative Scriptures. The opening lines allude to Adam and Eve's disobedience to God, Moses's receiving the law on Sinai, Christ's redemption of mankind, the Holy Spirit as divine inspiration for the Scriptures, and the creation story. Besides the book of Genesis, where the familiar creation and fall are recorded, the poet alludes to 14 other biblical passages in the first 13 lines alone.

Although Milton's care in closely echoing his biblical source is an impressive achievement, he often deviates from that source. There is, for example, no direct biblical statement that affirms Milton's implication that the fallen angels later became heathen gods.

Osiris, Isis, and Orus, classical Egyptian deities, are not mentioned in the Bible. In the opening lines, Milton follows his biblical

source explicitly, however, when he asks the Spirit to instruct him, he says "for thou know'st; Thou from the first/ Wast present." These lines are a combination of two sources that read "the things of God knoweth no man, but the Spirit of God (I Cor. 2:11) and when the earth was "without form and void . . . the Spirit of God moved upon the face of the waters" (Gen. 1: 2). For the most part, *Paradise Lost* has been well received by orthodox Christians knowledgeable about the Bible.

Study Questions

1. What is Milton's main purpose or theme of his epic poem?

2. What is the setting of the opening scene of the poem?

3. Who is next in command to the archangel Satan?

4. What is Satan's attitude in the beginning of the poem?

5. In what way does Milton's enumeration of his fallen angels resemble Homer's *Iliad*?

6. Who leads the fallen angels to dig for gold in Hell? Why?

7. What is the name of the temple that rose out of the ground in Hell?

8. According to Milton, what had many of the pagan gods been before the history of Man?

9. What are Milton's basic sources for *Paradise Lost*?

10. What is the plan of action for the fallen angels and their leaders at the end of Book I?

Answers

1. Milton intends to "justify the ways of God to men."

2. Satan and his angels are chained to the burning lake of fire in Hell.

3. Beelzebub is next in command to Satan.

4. Satan is sure that, in spite of his present state in Hell, he will never bow to God.

5. The list of Milton's fallen angels is an epic convention that resembles the catalogue of ships in Homer's *Iliad*.

6. Mammon leads the fallen angels to dig for gold in Hell. He wants Hell to equal Heaven in riches.

7. The temple was called Pandemonium and served as Satan's capitol in Hell.

8. Milton states that the pagan deities had once been demons in Hell and, before their rebellion, angels in Heaven.

9. Milton uses the epic poem, emulating Homer and Virgil. He alludes to the Bible and classical literature for his subject and characterization.

10. Satan and his angels gather in his capitol, Pandemonium, to discuss what they will do to avenge God.

Suggested Essay Topics

1. Satan is often seen as an attractive character in *Paradise Lost.* In what way could he be perceived as attractive? Discuss Milton's involvement with the character of Satan. Does he identify with Satan? What statement is Milton making about the fallen archangel? Cite examples from the poem to support your answer.

2. Milton declares that his poem will pursue "Things unattempted yet in prose or rhyme." Discuss these words in light of the subject matter of the poem. Why did Milton consider his poem superior to those of Homer and Virgil? Discuss the superiority of his subject matter. Use examples from the poem to support your ideas.

Book II

New Characters:

Sin: *Satan's daughter, born out of his head in Heaven*

Death: *born as the son of Satan and Sin's incestuous relationship*

Chaos: *rules the region of confusion between Hell and Earth*

Night: *the consort of Chaos*

Summary

As he is ready to begin the consultation, Satan sits on his exalted throne in Pandemonium, the capitol of Hell. Addressing his angels as "Powers, Dominions, and Deities," Satan, in his vanity, is comparable to the monarchs of the Orient. He assures them that Heaven is not lost, and with a spirit of unity, they can return again to claim their "just inheritance." He offers the alternatives of "open war" or "covert guile" as he opens the debate with an invitation to anyone who wishes to speak.

Moloch, the strongest and fiercest demon, begins the debate with a proposal for "open war." His hopes for equality with God have been dashed, and his despair has fuelled his desire for revenge. He argues that it would be better to be reduced to nonexistence than to bear the pain of their present state in Hell with no hope of an end to their suffering. Since nothing could be worse, they have nothing to lose by defying God openly. He insists that if the fallen angels are "indeed divine" and cannot be annihilated, God can do no more to them than he has already done. In his desperation for revenge, Moloch advocates that they alarm and disturb God though they will never be victorious since Heaven is inaccessible to them.

Belial, though false, is a much more humane and dignified demon who opposes Moloch's plan and proposes peace at all costs. He too is aware that God could destroy them completely, but, unlike Moloch, he feels it would be better to exist in Hell than "to be no more." In skillful debate, he exposes the folly of Moloch's argument and reminds the fallen angels that Heaven is closely guarded and "impregnable." He insists that Hell could get worse if they

would arouse God to even greater condemnation and reasons that God might "remit his anger" and soften their punishment if they do not provoke him. Belial also suggests that familiarity with the horror and darkness of Hell will eventually lessen the pain.

Mammon speaks next, advocating that they stay in Hell rather than risk spending eternity in forced subjection to Heaven's supreme Lord whom they hate. He reminds them that in Hell they will be free of God, choosing "hard liberty" rather than the "easy yoke" of servility. Pointing out that Hell can equal Heaven in gems and gold, he questions Heaven's appeal. He concludes his speech, advising a dismissal of all ideas about war against Heaven. Mammon's proposal is well received by the legions of angels who applaud loudly in approval. With the threatening sword of the heavenly angel Michael still vivid in their memory, many of them dread going to war against Heaven.

The last to speak, Beelzebub, second only to Satan in power, captivates his audience with his broad Atlas shoulders and majestic appearance. Since they have voted to stay in Hell, Beelzebub addresses the fallen angels by their new titles as Princes of Hell. He warns them to make no mistake about God's intentions. He has doomed them to this place as their "dungeon" not their "safe retreat," as some might think, and he rules them with an iron sceptor. Beelzebub exposes the folly of discussing peace or war since war against Heaven has already determined their irreversible fate. He proposes another plan, involving the new world God has created which is the happy seat of the race called Man. Beelzebub reasons that this place, possibly within their reach, may hold opportunities for revenge against God by destroying his new world or claiming it as their own and driving out God's new inhabitants. It was Satan, the poet says, who first devised the devious scheme against mankind, and Beelzebub simply acts as his mouthpiece in the devilish council.

After the fallen angels vote to approve Beelzebub's proposal, he calls for a volunteer to search for this newly created world. The journey entails innumerable hazards involved in traveling through the vast, bottomless Abyss that is heavily guarded by sentries of angels. All hope rests on the responsible one who will volunteer to go. After a long silence, Satan proudly volunteers, conscious of the honor he will receive. Announcing quickly that he will go alone, he avoids the threat of a possible rival who might offer to go and, thereby, thwart his plan for his own personal ambition. Seeing it as an act of self-sacrifice, however, his followers deify him, rising and bowing to him with "awful reverence."

The council is dissolved as they bid farewell to Satan, their brave chief, with thunderous shouts and the blasts of trumpets. Though their hopes have been temporarily raised, they become sad and perplexed as soon as Satan leaves. To overcome their "restless thoughts," they form small groups, entertaining themselves with athletic games, the singing of songs, and irrelevant philosophical debates concerning good and evil. Some explore the geographic regions of Hell to see whether they can discover an "easier habitation" but find only a perverted and monstrous nature where "life dies" and "death lives."

In the meantime, Satan approaches the gates of Hell where he meets a woman, whose name is Sin, holding the key. She is fair to the waist but otherwise resembles a foul, scaly serpent surrounded with barking Hell-hounds that freely pass in and out of her womb. She was born full-grown out of the head of Satan when he first planned his rebellion against God in Heaven. Guarding the other side of the gate is a shapeless creature who approaches Satan, threatening to drive him back to Hell. Satan confronts him, but just as they are ready to fight, Sin rushes between them, telling Satan that it is his own son, Death. Born out of the incestuous union of Satan and Sin, Death, in turn, has raped Sin, and the barking monsters are the fruits of the second incestuous act.

After Sin's forewarning, Satan softens his approach and finally convinces her to open the gates of Hell and let him pass. She opens them but is unable to close them again. Passing through the vast Abyss, Satan comes upon the throne of Chaos and his consort, Night. He informs them of his plan and asks them to direct his course to Earth. Chaos encourages him, telling him it is not far. Continuing his upward flight, Satan encounters many difficulties. Meanwhile, Sin and Death have been following his track, paving a broad and well-worn highway and bridge over the Abyss for easy access from Hell to Earth. Satan finally comes within view of Earth, which hangs by a golden chain from Heaven, and his mind fills with "mischievous revenge."

Analysis

Satan begins the infernal consultation as he opens the debate by feigning a choice between "open war" and "covert guile" for the recovery of Heaven. It is learned later, when Beelzebub addresses the council, however, that the debate has been skillfully manipulated by Satan. Beelzebub is the last to speak, and he echoes Satan's own plan of avenging God by harming his new creation, Man. Beelzebub's proposal, the poet says, was "first devised by Satan." In Book I, Satan had already suggested the strategy of guile rather than force to accomplish the purpose of revenge.

> Henceforth his might we know, and know our own,
> So as not either to provoke, or dread
> New war provoked; our better part remains
> To work in close design, by fraud or guile
> What force effected not.
>
> P. L., I, 643–47

Rumor has it that God intends to create a new world and a new race. Since God is now inaccessible to them, their alternate plan of revenge, Satan says, should be to corrupt the work of the "great Creator."

Many Renaissance poets held the belief that the creation of Man preceded Satan's rebellion in Heaven. They believed it was Satan's jealousy of the newly created Adam that prompted the archangel's revolt against God in Heaven which led to his subsequent fall. Milton took the view less prevalent in his time. His Satan rebels against the Son's recent advancement in Heaven which threatens to usurp the archangel's power. Though Satan's rebellion against God is not merely a sudden unexplainable act of pride, his motives are selfish and his actions are ludicrous in light of the fact that he is asked to obey and show reverence to an inherently superior being, the Son of God. Stella Purce Revard justifies Milton's choice on the grounds that his "Satan evokes less sympathy from the reader with his refusal to bow the knee to the Son" than does the Satan of other Renaissance poets who depict his refusal to bow to Adam, an inferior being.

In *Paradise Lost*, Satan realizes that Man will be "favored more/ Of him who rules above," but his jealousy of Adam and Eve does not come to the foreground until after the archangel has left Hell and sees them in their blissful state in Paradise. "What do mine eyes with grief behold" (P. L., IV, l. 358).

Some critics believe that the demons who speak in the devilish council parallel the people Milton observed when he attended sessions at the Council of State. One can readily see that they frequently demonstrate human characteristics as they rationalize their points of view. Moloch is a typical die-hard who stubbornly refuses to abandon the idea of his former position in Heaven. Ready to fight, he resists any other alternative and is willing to be annihilated rather than accept his present fate in Hell. Belial, though "false and hollow," is a skillful debater, turning Moloch's argument against him point by point. In contrast to Moloch, Belial is a peacemaker and makes "the worse appear/ The better reason." Mammon does not want to go back to Heaven if it will entail the singing of "forced halleluiahs" to God. He prefers "hard liberty" to the "easy yoke" of servility. In the case of Mammon, Milton expresses his own views through the words of a demon. This is reminiscent of his reference to governmental corruption in *Samson Agonistes*.

> But what more oft in nations grown corrupt,
> And by their vices brought to servitude,
> Than to love bondage more than liberty,
> Bondage with ease than strenuous liberty.
>
> *Samson Agonistes*, 268–71

Milton seems to identify more closely with Mammon, who advocates action, than with Belial, who simply yields to "peaceful sloth." The debate of the devilish council steadily improves as each speaker becomes more rational, slowly relinquishing the idea of the recovery of Heaven as they realize its futility. Beelzebub speaks last, drawing the group together with his proposal of a counter plan that involves spying on God's newly created world and contriving a guileful act of revenge.

Biblical allusions abound in *Paradise Lost*. Ironically, Beelzebub's argument to the demons in the council is shot through with references to the Scriptures.

> For he, be sure,
> In height or depth, still first and last will reign
> Sole king, and of his kingdom lose no part
> By our revolt, but over Hell extend
> His empire, and with iron scepter rule
> Us here, as with his golden those in Heaven.
>
> P. L., II, 323–28

Beelzebub's words allude to the risen Christ in the book of Revelation. "I am Alpha and Omega, the first and the last" (Rev. 1:11). God, Beelzebub says, will rule as "Sole King" which alludes to the "King of kings, and Lord of lords" in I Timothy 6:15. The Bible makes several references to the "iron scepter" with which the Son of God will rule after Satan has been defeated. The prophecy concerning the heathen is given in the Psalms. "Thou shalt break them with a rod of iron; thou shalt dash them in pieces like a potter's vessel" (Ps. 2:9). Another prophecy from Psalms 45:6 reads: "Thy throne, O God, is for ever and ever; the sceptre of thy kingdom is a right sceptre." In view of the Scriptures, Beelzebub is, unknowingly, prophesying his own doom in these lines.

Besides his heavy reliance on the Bible, Milton's classical allusions are also woven throughout his epic poem. The character of Sin, who was "woman to the waist, and fair,/ But ended foul in many a scaly fold," is patterned after Scylla in Virgil's *Aeneid*.

> . . . to the waist
> A maiden she, with comely-fashioned breast,
> Her after-part a sea-thing monster-sized
> With dolphin tails on wolfish belly fixed.
>
> *Aeneid*, iii, 428–31

Sin's origins also reflect those of classical myth. She was born out of the head of Satan ("a goddess armed/ Out of thy head I sprung") just as Athena, in Greek myth, sprang fully armed from the head of Zeus.

As the group of fallen angels explore the geographic regions of Hell, they find an area described as "Burns frore (frozen), and cold performs the effect of fire" (P. L. II, 595). With his frequent use of oxymoron, Milton emphasizes certain passages by bringing the contradictory terms together. Other examples of this rhetorical antithesis are "darkness visible" (I, 63) and "for evil only good" (II, 623).

After his exhaustive journey through Chaos, Satan nears the "pendant world." He sees the world (Earth) as a star of "smallest magnitude." His view of the entire universe gives an impression of distance that is contradictory to that of Book I where Hell is "as far removed from God . . . / As from the center thrice to the utmost pole" (P. L., I, 74). When we consider that Sin and Death are building a bridge from the gates of Hell to Earth, our former impression of the vast distance that the angels have fallen from Heaven to Hell shrinks in our imagination.

Study Questions

1.   What does Moloch propose at the devilish council?

2.   How does Belial's proposal compare to Moloch's?

3.   What is Mammon's argument at the council?

4.   Who is Beelzebub, and what does he propose?

5.   Who volunteers to go alone to spy on God's new creation?

6.   What is the volunteer's true motive for his seemingly sacrificial act of exploring God's new world?

7.   Who does Satan meet at the gates of Hell?

8.   Where did the barking Hell-hounds originate?

9.   After which classical figure does Milton pattern the character of Sin?

10.   Whom does Satan meet as he travels through the vast Abyss on his way to Earth?

Answers

1.   Moloch proposes open war and is willing to risk annihilation in the attempt at armed conflict to avenge God.

2. Belial opposes Moloch's plan. He advocates peace at all costs, reasoning that God might soften their punishment if they do not provoke him further.

3. Mammon wants to stay in Hell where he will be free of God. He chooses "hard liberty" rather than the "easy yoke" of servility.

4. Beelzebub is the mouthpiece for Satan himself. He proposes a plan to avenge God through his new creation, Man.

5. Satan volunteers to go to Earth to spy on God's new race.

6. Satan is interested in his own honor and personal ambition.

7. Satan meets his daughter, Sin, and their son, Death.

8. Death raped his own mother, Sin, and she gave birth to the Hell-hounds, the fruits of the incestuous act.

9. Milton patterns Sin after Scylla in Virgil's *Aeneid.* Also, both Sin and Athena (in Greek myth) were born fully armed out of the heads of their fathers (Satan and Zeus).

10. Satan meets Chaos sitting on his throne, along with his consort, Night.

Suggested Essay Topics

1. Commentators have compared the debate in the devilish council to sessions of the Council of State in Milton's day. In what way do Moloch, Belial, Mammon, and Beelzebub portray human characteristics? Compare and contrast their points of view. Do they all have one common goal? Support your answer with examples from the poem.

2. Satan volunteers to go on a journey that entails innumerable hazards. What can he hope to gain from this supposed act of self-sacrifice? How is this act typical of his character? Why does he choose to go alone? Why would another volunteer spoil his plan? Give examples from the poem to support your view.

Book III

New Characters:

God: *creator of Heaven, the new world (Earth), and a new race called Man*

The Son: *sits on the right hand of God, the Father; volunteers to go down to Earth and give his life as a ransom for Man's sins*

Uriel: *the angel of the sun; one of seven archangels who stands ready at God's command*

Summary

The poet opens Book III with an invocation to "holy Light," the essence of God. "Since God is light," it has coexisted with him eternally and flows from His very being. This light, the poet says, was the first thing to appear in God's creation, emanating from him as the "offspring of Heaven first-born." The poet has come out of utter darkness (Hell), passed through middle darkness (Chaos), and has now reached the safe environs of God's holy light. The poet is blind, however, and must depend solely on his inner vision for divine inspiration. He invokes the muse of Sion and visits the Scriptures nightly for spiritual enlightenment. In his blindness, he compares his fate to that of Thamyris, Homer (Maeonides), Tiresias, and Phineus and wishes to equal them in fame also. Since his blindness has cut him off from the book of "Nature's works," he asks that the divine light of inspiration grant him inner eyes that he might see and tell things that are invisible to other mortals.

The "Almighty Father" sits on his throne in Heaven with his Son on his right hand and a myriad of angels gathered around him as "thick as stars." From above, he views his entire creation at a glance and watches Adam and Eve in their happy state in Eden. As his eyes survey Hell and Chaos, he detects the figure of Satan who is preparing to land on God's newly created world. God perceives Satan's need for "desperate revenge" and predicts that Satan's lies to Man will cause him to transgress. He has these feelings with his Son. Breaking God's command and his pledge of obedience, Man and his progeny will fall through nobody's fault but their own since they have been given free will. All created beings were given free choice, God says, and cannot justly accuse their Maker of a predestined fate that has governed their condition.

Even though God possesses the foreknowledge of Man's fall and all other future events, he does not foreordain those events but allows freedom of choice to all created beings. The fallen angels erred by their own suggestion, God says, and will not be given grace. On the other hand, Man will be granted mercy and justice since his fall will be brought about by the deception of Satan.

As God speaks, an "ambrosial fragrance" wafts through the air, and the angels are filled with a new joy. The Son's face shines with a light of divine compassion, reflecting the love and grace of God, his Father.

The Son praises God's compassion for Man whose fall, "though joined/ With his own folly," will be artfully maneuvered by the fraudulent Satan. God is a wise judge, the Son says, who will not allow Satan, their Adversary, to draw the whole race of mankind into Hell with him and, thereby, thwart God's purpose.

God commends the Son for reflecting his Father's thoughts and assures him that Man will not be lost but will be given grace. He will be saved if he chooses, yet he will owe his deliverance to God who will place an "umpire Conscience" within the race of Man, warning them of their sinful state. This will be a reminder to them that they must pray, repent, and show obedience to God. Those who harden their hearts with neglect and scorn will be excluded from God's mercy.

There can be no justice, however, unless someone is willing to pay the ultimate price, his life as a ransom for Man's sins. God calls for a volunteer, but the heavenly choir stands mute. Out of the silence the Son of God speaks, offering to go down to Earth and die for the sake of Man. The Son has the assurance that he will not stay in the grave but will "rise victorious" and conquer his enemy, Death. He promises to bind the "powers of darkness" and lead the redeemed to Heaven where there shall be no clouds of anger but only joy in God's presence.

The Son is now silent, but his face shines with "immortal love/ To mortal men." All the heavenly angels are filled with admiration, wondering what this might mean. God explains that the Son will become a man, born "by wondrous birth" to a virgin as one of

Adam's descendants. Through Adam all men will die, but through the Son all who renounce their unrighteous deeds and receive new life will be saved. By descending to the nature of Man, the Son will not be degraded, however. Because he has offered to leave his throne in Heaven to save the world, the Son has been found to be worthy of maintaining the position of the Son of God. Love, rather than birthright, has proven his true merit. Through humility he has been exalted to the throne and shall reign as Son of both God and Man. In the last days, he will appear in the sky and judge the living and the dead from past ages. The wicked shall sink into Hell that will thereafter be sealed. A new Heaven and Earth will spring from the ashes of the burning world. Here the just will dwell, seeing golden days when Joy, Love, and Truth will be triumphant.

The Almighty instructs the angels to adore the Son and honor him as God's equal. Loud hosannas fill the air and the heavenly angels cast down their crowns in adoration of the Son. They then raise their harps and crown their heads again, preparing to play a symphony in adoration of their Omnipotent and Eternal King. Songs of praise are addressed to the Son for overthrowing the warring angels in Heaven. By contrast, in his life on Earth the Son will put an end to strife among men by his own example of mercy, justice, and divine love.

In the meantime, Satan alights on the uninhabited world, a boundless continent of "dark, waste, and wild" land where storms out of Chaos are an ever-present threat. Walking alone, he finds no sign of life. This is the place where men's works of vanity, such as the Tower of Babel, will be built in the future. It will be called the "Paradise of Fools" where people mistake outward forms of religion for true faith.

As Satan walks in search of Paradise, he reaches a magnificent stairway to Heaven that resembles Jacob's ladder in the Old Testament. Underneath the stairs flows a sea of jasper and liquid pearl. The stairs are let down, but it aggravates Satan since he is excluded from the entrance to his former home in Heaven. From the lower stairs, Satan suddenly discovers a wide passage continuing down to Earth.

Satan winds his way down with ease, but he approaches other worlds and decides to land on the sun instead. He sees Uriel, the

angel of the sun, whose back is turned. Satan changes his shape to a "stripling Cherub" so he can ask Uriel the directions to Paradise. Satan deceives Uriel with hypocrisy when he tells the angel that he wants to see God's "wondrous work, chiefly Man" so he can glorify God. Uriel praises Satan's worthy intentions and points out Adam's bower in Paradise. Satan leaves, bowing low as he shows honor and reverence to a superior angel. Speedily, he flies toward Earth and lands on Mount Niphates.

Analysis

In Book III, the images of light in Heaven stand in marked contrast to the previous darkness of the infernal regions of Hell. Throughout the poem, symbols of darkness, repeatedly linked with descent or falling, stand diametrically opposed to visions of light that are reached only by the ascent to the celestial light. It is Satan's sin of pride that has caused his descent into darkness. He has fallen from "the happy realms of light" (P. L., I, 85) onto the "dreary plain . . . void of light (P. L., I, 180–82). By way of contrast, the heavenly angels sing praises to the Son "In whose conspicuous countenance . . . the Almighty Father shines" (P. L., III, 385–86). God's light shines through the Son, but Satan, who is absent from God, dwells in the darkness of Hell.

Having endured the abyss of "utter darkness," the poet now leads the reader upward through the area of "middle darkness" to the regions of God's "holy Light." In declaring that "God is Light," the poet borrows from the biblical text. "This then is the message which we have heard of him, and declare unto you, that God is light, and in him is no darkness at all (I John 1:5). God cannot be seen by any man, his essence being "unapproached light" that "Dwelt from eternity." The biblical source is found in I Timothy 6:16. "Who only hath immortality, dwelling in the light which no man can approach unto; whom no man hath seen, nor can see." Later, the angels sing praises to the "Fountain of Light" (God) who is invisible in his glorious brightness, and whom they "Approach not" unless they "veil their eyes" with both wings.

Though the poet's "dark descent" into Hell has been "hard and rare," he now feels safe as he re-ascends into the realm of God's light, but, ironically, he is blind. Dolefully, he grieves his loss of sight as he reflects on nature.

> Thus with the year
> Seasons return; but not to me returns
> Day, or the sweet approach of even or morn,
> Or sight of vernal bloom, or summer's rose,
> Or flocks, or herds, or human face divine;
> But cloud instead.
>
> P. L., III, 40–45

He has been shunned from "the book of knowledge fair." Since the days of Aristotle, people had believed that knowledge was to be acquired through nature. Sight was, therefore, a necessity for the observation of the beauty of the seasons, the changes of day and night, the varieties of plants and animals, and the "human face divine." Since wisdom through physical sight is "quite shut out," the poet will explore the mind's inward eyes so that he might see "things invisible to mortal sight."

Milton's use of the epic simile is an effective comparison between the stairway to Heaven, encountered by Satan on his way to Eden, and the biblical story of Jacob's ladder. "The stairs were such as whereon Jacob saw/ Angels ascending and descending, bands/ Of guardians bright, when he from Esau fled." In the biblical account, Jacob is fleeing to avoid being killed after he has deceived Isaac by impersonating his brother, Esau. Falling asleep, Jacob "dreamed, and behold a ladder set up on the earth, and the top of it reached to heaven: and behold the angels of God ascending and descending on it" (Gen. 28:12). Though the imagery is comparable, Satan and Esau are depicted with opposing characteristics. When Esau sees the stairway in his dream, he is filled with fear and reverence to God. But when Satan sees it, he simply stands on the "lower stair" and is filled with envy as he catches sight of the fair World that God has created for Man.

In *Paradise Lost*, God is, paradoxically, "unapproached light," yet Milton draws him as a character who carries on a conversation with his Son. Though some commentators have interpreted the dialogue between God and the Son in Book III as mere theological dogma, a mouthpiece for Milton, Irene Samuel, refutes this idea, arguing that readers have "misconstrued as dogma what Milton intended as drama" (Irene Samuel, *The Dialogue in Heaven: A Reconsideration of Paradise Lost*, p. 235). Milton sets the scene for the dramatic interchange between God and the Son by contrasting the "holy Light" of Heaven to the "utter darkness" and "middle darkness" of the first two books.

God, being omniscient, immediately sees Satan who is loose in the universe and bent on "desperate revenge." In a rather prosaic way, God voices his foreknowledge of the fact that Satan will falsely pervert mankind with his guile, causing Man to fall. God informs the Son and the angels that he created Man and all "Ethereal Powers . . . Sufficient to have stood, though free to fall." In this way, God has the assurance of the "true allegiance" of the faithful ones.

In his benevolence, God announces to the Son and the crowd of angels in Heaven that Man, deceived by Satan, "shall find grace." The Son responds with passionate praise to the Father not merely for the love and justice he shows to Man, but also for his resistance to Satan's devious plan of drawing all of mankind into Hell and, thereby, thwarting God's purposes. Though he speaks with respect and reverence, the Son, displaying an independent spirit, informs God that allowing Satan to carry out his revenge would have invited much-deserved criticism of the "goodness" and "greatness" of God.

God continues, telling the Son and the angels that someone must pay the price for Man's sins. God asks for a volunteer to go down to Earth and become Man. The Son offers to give his life as a ransom for Man's sin. He will break the bonds of Death, returning to Heaven with the multitude of the redeemed to live forever in peace and joy. This is reminiscent of the infernal council in Hell when a volunteer is needed to spy on God's new creation, Man. Satan volunteers, but his purpose, in contrast to the Son's, is his own ambition for power. He would rather "reign in Hell, than serve in Heaven" (P. L., I, 263). Satan's offer, unlike the Son's, has been contrived and is manipulated by Beelzebub who simply echoes Satan's own original plan. When the Son humbly volunteers to descend to Earth and give his life as a ransom for Man's sin, he is exalted through his humility. God promises that the Son's nature will not be degraded. "Therefore thy humiliation shall exalt/ With thee thy manhood also to this throne." When Satan proudly volunteers to go to Earth, he is, by contrast to the Son, humiliated. In his desperate attempt to exalt himself, Satan later arrives in Pandemonium, boasting about his "success against Man" but instead of applause, he is, ironically, degraded when he is met with the general hiss of serpents (P. L., X, "The Argument").

In the dialogue between God and the Son, Milton reveals his theological views concerning the salvation of mankind. At the heart of his beliefs is the idea that Man was created with free will. God says, "I formed them free, and free they must remain." Though Man's salvation comes through God's grace, God makes it clear that to be saved requires Man's willingness. "Man shall not quite be lost, but sav'd who will,/ Yet not of will in him, but grace in me/ Freely vouchsafed." God declares that nobody can be reprobated unless they do not repent of their sins.

When Satan leaves the stairway to Heaven, he decides to alight on the sun where he will ask Uriel, the angel of the sun, to direct him toward Eden. Satan quickly changes into a stripling Cherub so Uriel will not recognize him as a demon escaped from Hell. Lying to Uriel, Satan tells the angel that he wants to find God's newest creation so he can admire them and send his praise and honor to God, their creator. Uriel believes the story of the "false dissembler," the poet says, since neither angels nor Man can recognize hypocrisy. It is "the only evil that walks/ Invisible, except to God alone."

Study Questions

1. What is the symbolic significance of the image of light in Book III?

2. Why is God referred to as "unapproached light"?

3. Whom does God point out to the Son as their dialogue begins?

4. Who answers God's call for a volunteer to die for Man's sins?

5. What is Jacob's ladder in the biblical account?

6. How does Satan's attitude toward God compare to Jacob's as they each view the "stairway to Heaven"?

7. Who is Uriel? What does Satan ask of him?

8. Why does Satan disguise himself when he meets Uriel?

9. Why does the poet lament the fact that he finds "no dawn"?

10. Why does the poet compare himself to Homer (Maeonides)?

Answers

1. The image of light represents the essence of God because "God is light."

2. God is "unapproached light" because no man has seen, nor is able to see Him.

3. God points to Satan who is nearing the wall of Heaven. God perceives Satan's plan of revenge that will cause Man to fall.

4. The Son offers to go down to Earth and become a man who will give his life as a ransom for Man's sin.

5. In a dream, Jacob sees a ladder that leads to Heaven with angels ascending and descending.

6. Jacob is filled with fear and reverence toward God, but Satan only feels envy when he sees God's new world.

7. Uriel is the angel of the sun. Satan asks Uriel the direction to Paradise.

8. Satan disguises himself to avoid being recognized as a demon from Hell.

9. The poet (Milton) is blind.

10. Homer is also an epic poet who shares Milton's fate of being blind.

Suggested Essay Topics

1. The poet begins Book III with an invocation to "holy Light." In what way is God symbolic of light? How is light the very essence of God? Was light created by God? Has it existed from the beginning? In what way is the "holy Light" symbolically significant to the Son? To the angels? To Man? Cite examples from the poem to support your views.

2.   The Son offers to go down to Earth to die for Man's sin. Compare and contrast this with the call for volunteers in the infernal consultation in Hell. How do Satan and the Son compare as volunteers in a dangerous mission? Contrast their motives. What do each of them hope to gain? Do each of them offer hope? Support your argument with examples from the poem.

Book IV

New Characters:

Adam: *first man created by God; forbidden to eat the fruit of the Tree of Knowledge in Paradise*

Eve: *first woman created by God out of Adam's rib; tempted by the Serpent to eat the forbidden fruit*

Gabriel: *an angel guarding the gate of Paradise*

Uzziel: *an angel, who is next to Gabriel in power, guarding Paradise*

Ithuriel: *an angel appointed by Gabriel to search for Satan in Paradise*

Zephon: *an angel who helps Ithuriel find Satan and bring him to Gabriel for questioning*

Summary

Satan has reached the top of Mount Niphates which overlooks Eden. As he anticipates his "bold enterprise" against God and Man, he is suddenly plagued with doubt and despair. Though he has escaped from his physical Hell, he has brought his inner Hell with him, admitting that "I myself am Hell." Sadly, he looks down at Eden, a pleasant place, and then at Heaven where the sun shines like the radiance of a god who holds dominion over the new world (Eden). Satan blames the sun whose brilliancy reminds him of his own lost glory in Heaven. He confesses it was his pride and ambition that caused him to wage war against Heaven's King. Acknowledging him as his creator, Satan concedes that God was undeserving of his rebellious actions. He reflects on God's goodness and feels that he owed him the praise and thanks that was due to him. Admitting his free will to stand or fall, he realizes he was treated justly. Unable to escape his miserable existence, he cries out for pardon, but only for a moment. He disdains submission to God and dreads the shame he would suffer among the spirits in Hell if he would admit that he could not subdue the Omnipotent. Concluding that "all good to me is lost," he decides that evil will be his good, and at least he will reign over more than half the world.

Meanwhile, unknown to Satan, Uriel, whose eyes have been following him since he left the sun, suddenly notices his disfigured body showing through his disguise.

Satan moves on to "delicious Paradise" that is surrounded by a high wall with an eastern gate. Above the wall he can see the trees laden with blossoms and fruit. As he approaches, the air becomes purer. Finding no entrance, he leaps over the wall and lands on the ground in Eden. Changing his appearance to a bird, he alights in the Tree of Life that is next to the Tree of Knowledge.

Ingulfed underneath Eden is a river flowing south and rising up as a "fresh fountain" that divides into four main streams to water all of the garden. Eden is a peaceful place filled with flowers, roses without thorns, cool caves, luxurious vines, and waterfalls. Satan sees many kinds of creatures but only two who stand "erect and tall." Spotting Adam and Eve, he realizes they have been created "God-like erect" in the "image of their glorious Maker." The naked pair were not created equal. Adam was formed for contemplation and valor, the poet says, and Eve was made for "softness" and "sweet attractive grace." The earthly pair walk hand in hand until they find a green shady spot bedecked with flowers next to a "fresh fountain" where they eat their supper of fruits as the beasts are frisking around them.

Irritated by Adam and Eve's idyllic happy life that contrasts sharply with his own, Satan plots his act of guile which will cause them to fall. Though they are not his direct enemies, he will avenge God by corrupting them and, thereby, enlarge his empire in Hell. In an attempt to get a closer look at the human pair, Satan alights from the tree and changes his shape, first to a lion, then to a tiger. When Adam speaks, Satan is all ears. Adam tells Eve that the Power that raised them from the dust must be infinitely good since all he requires of them is to refrain from eating the fruit of the Tree of Knowledge. Having given the earthly pair the power to rule over all creatures of the Earth, air, and sea, God asks for only one sign of their obedience. Death will be the penalty if they disobey by partaking of the forbidden fruit, but it is an easy prohibition since there is an abundance of other fruits in the garden.

Eve agrees that Adam is right. She then reminisces about the day she met Adam when she was first given life. After she awoke, she gazed into the lake and saw another shape that imitated her actions. She would still be there, she says, if a voice had not warned her that the image she was seeing was her own. The voice led her to Adam, but when she saw him, she turned to go back, finding the image in the lake more attractive. Adam convinced her to stay, and she yielded to his "manly grace." The Devil (Satan) turns aside, envious as Adam and Eve embrace.

Satan has heard them talking and decides to convince them to seek the knowledge that is forbidden. He must persuade them to eat the fruit, but first he will gather more information from the heavenly spirits who might be wandering around the garden.

At sunset the angel Gabriel, chief of the heavenly guards, sits at the eastern gate of Paradise when, suddenly, Uriel glides down to Earth on a sunbeam. He warns Gabriel of the evil spirit who might be lurking in Eden. Uriel relates the details of his earlier meeting with a spirit whom he has been watching from his sentry position in the sun. He has lost sight of him and fears there is trouble ahead unless someone finds him. Gabriel assures Uriel he will be found by morning, and the angel of the sun returns to his appointed post in the sun.

Night falls, and Adam reminds Eve that God has devised day and night, appointing a time for labor and rest. They must now go to sleep so they can rise again at dawn and attend to their garden. Eve asks Adam why the moon and stars shine all night when all else in God's creation sleeps. Adam replies that the planets must revolve around the Earth to give light to "nations yet unborn." Millions of God's spiritual creatures roam the Earth, keeping watch all night long. Sometimes one can hear their "celestial voices" singing in the "midnight air." Hand in hand, Adam and Eve retire to their "blissful bower," chosen by God who framed the trees, bushes, and fragrant flowers for their "delightful use." In their awe of Man, the birds, beasts, and insects dare not enter the bower. Before Adam and Eve enter, they send up a prayer of adoration and praise to God.

The poet praises "wedded Love," instituted by God as the "true source/ Of human offspring" and contrasts it to the "bought smile/ Of harlots." The poet also pronounces that it is the work of the devil, "our destroyer," to attack wedded love by advocating abstinence. As the happy pair sleep, Gabriel, heeding Uriel's warning, sends out his guards to find the fallen angel who has escaped from Hell. Two of the guards, Ithuriel and Zephon, find him squatting like a toad at Eve's ear, disturbing her dreams. Ithuriel touches Satan lightly with his spear. Startled, Satan springs up, revealing his true shape. When the angels question Satan's identity, he scoffs at them, reminding them that he outranked them in Heaven. Zephon tells Satan he is no longer recognizable since now he resembles his foul sin.

The guards bring Satan to Gabriel for questioning. Gabriel asks him why he has broken the bounds of Hell to come to Earth, and Satan replies that he has come to escape the pain. Gabriel questions him further, asking why he did not bring all of the fallen angels with him. Satan replies that he has been sent on a dangerous mission as a scout to explore a "better abode" for his legions of angels in Hell. Calling him a liar, Gabriel orders him to leave while the angels threaten him with spears. Disaster is prevented by a sign from God in Heaven, and Gabriel reminds Satan that both of them stand powerless without God. Murmuring, Satan flees from Eden.

Analysis

In Satan's opening soliloquy on Mount Niphates, his outwardly pompous behavior has given way to the private disclosure of his inner torment. His ambivalence controls the "Hell within him," leaving him powerless to escape his miserable existence. He concedes that God created him and was, therefore, undeserving of his rebellion, yet his pride will not allow him to submit to God and give up his position as the Prince of Hell. He curses God's love but then curses himself since he must now bear the just penalty of his

freely chosen actions against God. He fears that "feigned submission" would only lead to a "worse relapse." In desperation, he decides that all hope for good is lost, thus evil must be his good. Feeling powerless when he is in the presence of good, he admits that evil is the only thing he can achieve.

Satan's soliloquy reveals him as a villain who chooses evil but whose "practised falsehood" must, nevertheless, be presented "under saintly show." This is reminiscent of the soliloquies of Shakespeare's villains. In *Othello*, the character of Iago resembles Satan as the "artificer of fraud" when he deceives Othello into thinking that his wife, Desdemona, has been unfaithful to him. Speaking to himself, Iago admits his hypocrisy.

> How am I then a villain?
> Divinity of Hell!
> When devils will the blackest sins put on,
> They do suggest at first with heavenly shows,
> As I do now.
>
> *Othello*, II, iii, 348–53

Iago's plans to turn Desdemona's "virtue into pitch," is comparable to Satan's plot involving the temptation and destruction of Adam and Eve. When the fact that Milton wrote Satan's speech as part of his earlier proposed dramatic version of *Paradise Lost* is considered, the dramatic quality of the soliloquy which emulates those of Shakespeare's villains can be understood. Shakespeare, like Milton, also wrote his verse in unrhymed iambic pentameter.

In his soliloquy, Satan's appearance changes as he speaks. "Each passion dimmed his face/ Thrice changed with pale, ire, envy, and despair." He becomes increasingly "counterfeit" or hypocritical. The poet observes that "heavenly minds from such distempers foul/ Are ever clear." This is reminiscent of Virgil's *Aeneid*. After the poet has invoked the Muse, he questions "Juno's unrelenting wrath . . . In heavenly breasts do such fierce passions dwell?" (*Aeneid* I, 6, 16). It has been suggested by some commentators that Milton was alluding to these lines since he also uses the same idea later in the poem: "In heavenly spirits could such perverseness dwell" (P. L., VI, 788) from the war in Heaven, and "can envy dwell/ In heavenly breasts?" (P. L., IX, 729–30) from Satan's temptation of Eve. We know from Milton himself that he is emulating "Homer in Greek" and "Virgil in Latin."

In Book IV and throughout the rest of the poem, Milton distinguishes between the capabilities and obligations of the sexes. They are not equal, the poet says, and the "absolute rule" belongs to the male while the female yields in "subjection" to him. In the awareness of the seventeenth century, Milton's commonly accepted view would have been considered not only biblical but Aristotelian in that this is how Aristotle described the hierarchical order of nature. Aristotle himself declares that "between male and female the former is by nature superior and ruler, the latter inferior and subject" (Aristotle, *Politics*, I, v). When Milton says, "He for God only, she for God in him," the biblical allusion is clear. " . . . he is the image and glory of God: but the woman is the glory of the man . . . Neither was the man created for the woman; but the woman for the man" (I Cor. 11:7, 9). In the light of the theological dogma of Milton's day, women were granted an honorable position in society. Helen Gardner, commenting on Milton's view of male/female status in this passage, sees little difference between Milton and other writers of his age, particularly John Donne, but she feels "we find much in Milton's theology repellent because he sets it out so clearly." In Milton's time, people's thinking centered around the idea that all beings were classified in a natural hierarchy, and, therefore, male and female could not be equal and one must rule. Modern-day beliefs of equality for all people have vastly altered perceptions of Milton's seventeenth-century ideas about sex roles.

Eve's account of her first day of creation alludes to Ovid's myth about Narcissus who is a handsome young man sought after by many women. He cares for none of them but falls in love with his own reflection in the pool instead. He pines away for the image of himself until he dies and is reincarnated as a Narcissus flower (Edith Hamilton, *Mythology*, 87–8). Eve also gazes into a pool and vainly admires her own reflection, but a voice leads her to Adam whom she perceives as less fair than her own image. As she turns away, Adam calls her back, telling her they are one flesh. She yields to him with gratitude, realizing that his "manly grace/ And wisdom"

far exceeds her beauty. This is a foreshadowing of the fall which is later brought about by Eve's inability to resist the Serpent's flattery and Adam's inability to resist Eve's love and beauty.

Milton's description of Paradise is artfully laced with classical allusions. From Greek mythology, the Three Graces are sister goddesses who dispense charm for the dance. Pan is the Greek god of woods, fields, and flocks. By including them, the poet enriches the beauty of the pastoral scene. Enna, a city in Sicily, is the place where Proserpine, from ancient Roman mythology, was raped as she was gathering flowers. She was the daughter of Ceres, the goddess of the underworld. In keeping with the epic tradition, Milton weaves stories of classical gods and demons through the epic poem.

Milton's love for Latinisms is evident in Book IV as it is throughout the epic. Before Satan's soliloquy, the poet describes him as "much revolving" (*multa volvens)* which means that he is doing much pondering. "Me miserable!" (*me miserum)* is another Latinism that describes Satan's state of mind. Amiable (*amabilis)* means beautiful, and irriguous (*irriguus)* is another word for well-watered valley. Milton's fascination with the sounds of language is occasionally seen in his play on words. Adam addresses Eve when he says, "Sole partner and sole part of all these joys." With the use of alliteration and repetition, the poet also emphasizes Satan's despair.

> Now conscience wakes despair
> That slumbered, wakes the bitter memory
> Of what he was, what is, and what must be
> Worse; of worse deeds worse sufferings must ensue.

In Satan's speech, as if to punctuate his mood, he again repeats that it was "worse ambition" that was his downfall.

Study Questions

1. What does Satan feel is his greatest fault?

2. How does Satan feel about his own free will?

3. Where does Satan (in the form of a bird) alight when he first enters Paradise?

4. What is God's only prohibition to Adam and Eve in the garden?

5. Which mythological character does Milton allude to in Eve's story of her first day on Earth?

6. In what forms does Satan appear in Paradise in Book IV.

7. Where do Adam and Eve sleep in Paradise?

8. How does Uriel travel from his post in the sun to Paradise when he comes to warn Gabriel about an evil spirit that is loose?

9. What does Satan tell Gabriel when he is asked why he has left Hell?

10. Why does Satan finally leave Paradise?

Answers

1. Satan feels that his pride and ambition have brought him down to his miserable state.

2. Satan feels that he has been created free to fall.

3. Satan alights in the Tree of Life as a cormorant or bird.

4. God prohibits Adam and Eve to eat the fruit of the Tree of Knowledge.

5. Eve's story, recalling her love for her own reflection, alludes to the classical myth of Narcissus.

6. Satan appears as a cormorant (bird) in the Tree of Life, a lion and tiger among the beasts, and a toad at Eve's ear.

7. Adam and Eve sleep in a bower prepared for them by God.

8. Uriel glides down to Earth on a sunbeam.

9. Satan tells Gabriel he has left Hell to escape the pain.

10. God sends a sign from Heaven, preventing disaster and showing both Gabriel and Satan that they are powerless without God.

Suggested Essay Topics

1. Milton first intended to use Satan's soliloquy in a dramatic presentation of *Paradise Lost*. Discuss the dramatic characterization in Satan's speech. In what ways do his words characterize Satan? What do we learn about Satan that we have not known thus far in the poem? Does his speech elicit our sympathy? Does it turn us against him? Cite examples from the poem to explain your answer.

2. God forbade Adam and Eve to eat the fruit of the Tree of Knowledge. Explain the symbolism inherent in God's prohibition. What would happen if they ate the fruit? How would it make them "Equal with Gods"? Give examples from the poem to support your argument.

Book V

New Characters:

Raphael: *God's angel; sent to Adam and Eve to warn them of the sin of disobedience to God*

Abdiel: *the only follower of Satan who remains faithful to God in the war in Heaven*

Summary

In the morning, Adam awakes to the sound of birds singing in the trees. He has slept well but is alarmed at the sight of Eve's disheveled look. Rousing her from a night of fitful sleep, Adam learns that she has had a disturbing dream. Someone, whose voice sounded like Adam's, had spoken into her ear, she says, asking her to join him during the moonlit hours to enjoy the cool and silent beauty of the night. She rose at Adam's call but did not see him. Searching for him, she found only the Tree of Knowledge that seemed fairer than it had in the light of day. Gazing at the tree stood a winged creature who vowed that no one would forbid him to taste its fruit. Without hesitation he picked and tasted the fruit as a "damp horror" ran through Eve's body. The creature held the fruit to her mouth, tempting her to eat and become a goddess. After she smelled the fruit, she was unable to resist. Immediately she began to fly through the air with him, but suddenly he was gone, and she sank down. She is now happy it has only been a dream.

Adam is uneasy about Eve's dream. He explains that though she was created pure and is, therefore, left untouched by her evil dream, Fancy or imagination often overrules Reason when a person sleeps, producing "wild work" from events of the past. Assuring her that their talk of the previous night has probably caused her dream, Adam is confident that evil "may come and go" into the mind and leave no trace. While awake, he says, she will never be as impetuous as she was in her dream. In spite of his encouragement, a "gentle tear" falls from her eye, but Adam kisses it away as they hurry to their work.

Before they begin their labors, however, they bow in adoration to God. Without ritual, words flow spontaneously from their lips. Glorifying God for his creation, they also praise him for his goodness and divine power. They call on the creatures of the Earth and all the planets and elements to join them in praise for their eternal God. Ending their morning prayer with an appeal for God's continuous bounty of good, they ask him to disperse any evil that might have been concealed during the night.

As Adam and Eve go about their morning tasks, God looks down upon them from Heaven with pity. He sends Raphael to Earth to caution them about the danger of Satan lurking in the garden and plotting their fall with his deceit and lies. Raphael is also instructed to remind them of their free will to choose between good and evil.

With haste, he leaves Heaven to deliver his urgent message. Admired by all winged creatures, he soars in the shape of a phoenix through the ethereal sky. He alights on the "eastern cliff of Paradise" and changes back to his proper shape, a six-winged seraph.

Spotting Raphael in the distance, Adam calls Eve to the opening of their bower to see the "glorious shape" approaching through the fields of sweet-smelling flowers and "spicy forest." He asks Eve to make preparations to entertain their guest. She quickly picks the choicest fruits of Paradise and strews the ground with rose

petals. Meanwhile, Adam fearlessly approaches Raphael with
stately solemnity, bowing with reverence as he comes near. Adam
invites Raphael to stay and eat with them; he accepts. Raphael hails
Eve as the "Mother of Mankind" whose fruitfulness will fill the
world. Their table is the "grassy turf," and their seats are made of
moss. Hesitantly, Adam shares his food with Raphael, fearing that
perhaps it would be unsavory to "spiritual natures." Raphael tells
Adam that angels require food and live by the five senses just as
humans do. He explains that all forms of life need food and there
is no sharp distinction between spirit and matter. Though Heaven's
trees bear fruit and its vines nectar, Raphael savors the unusual
varieties of fruits found in Eden. Eve, who is naked, fills their cups
with liquors, innocently ministering to their needs. In Paradise, the
poet says, love reigns without lust or jealousy.

Adam then decides he should not let this occasion pass without questioning his guest about Heaven and its inhabitants.
Raphael responds by depicting God as one who created all beings
with various forms and to varying degrees. He elaborately describes
the "scale of Nature" in which all created things have their place.
He explains that created beings are more spiritual as they become
proportionately nearer to God. "Differing but in degree" not in kind,
Raphael says, the human body may someday "turn all to spirit" if
Man is "found obedient." Adam is troubled by the condition of
obedience and asks Raphael to explain it further. Raphael warns
Adam that he must obey God's original command to abstain from
eating the fruit of the Tree of Knowledge. Though Adam was created perfect, he is not immutable. He has, however, been given free
will to choose his own destiny, Raphael says. He tells Adam that
some of the angels have already fallen into Hell because of their
disobedience to God.

Upon request, Raphael tells Adam what transpired in Heaven
when the angels fell as he relates the story of the war in Heaven.
Before the world was created and Chaos reigned, God called his
angels to his throne in Heaven to announce that he had that day
begotten a Son who now sits at his right hand. The Son has been
appointed their head to whom all knees should bow. Anyone who
disobeys the Son, also disobeys God and will be cast into utter
darkness forever.

All the angels seem pleased, spending their day in mystical dance that resembles the intricate mazes and divine harmony of the stars and planets. Their dance delights even God Himself. A table is set and the angels eat and drink in celebration of the good news. Night falls and the angels go to sleep, but Satan's pride and envy keep him awake. At midnight, he awakens his subordinate, Beelzebub, and speaks to him secretly. He asks him to assemble the legions of angels and tell them that Satan and all his followers have been ordered to go to the North to prepare to receive the great Messiah. Though Satan's words are a lie, his associate carries out his orders, and all obey Satan, their highly respected leader.

Meanwhile, God sees "rebellion rising" among Satan's legions of angels and warns the Son that Satan is erecting a power equal to theirs. He advises the Son to prepare for battle. The Son calmly replies that he is ready, with the power given to him by God, to subdue the rebels and "quell their pride."

In the meantime, Satan has already gathered his powers that are as numerous as the stars at night or the dewdrops in the morning. From his royal seat high on a hill, Satan addresses his angels by their princely titles. He tries to convince them that they will lose those titles and their freedom if they pay "knee-tribute" to both the Father and the Son.

Of all the myriads of angels, only Abdiel speaks out in defiance against Satan, accusing him of blasphemy, falsehood, and pride. Abdiel argues that God's decree is just, giving His only Son the right to rule with Him in Heaven. He questions Satan's right to challenge God who created him and "formed the powers of Heaven." God's law would not make the angels less but would "exalt" their "happy state" instead. He pleads with Satan to stop his "impious rage" and seek pardon from God before it is too late.

None of the angels stand by Abdiel which increases Satan's haughtiness even more. He refuses to acknowledge God as his creator, using the excuse that he does not remember when his Maker gave him being. He is "self-begot" and "self-raised," he says. Ordering Abdiel to leave, Satan's words are met with widespread applause from his legions of angels.

Abdiel, "though alone," is courageous and bold. Predicting Satan's fall, he tells him that he need no longer trouble himself with

escaping the yoke "of God's Messiah." He can soon expect to feel
God's wrath on his head at which point there will be no turning
back. Abdiel remains faithful and loyal to God. As he leaves, the
angels surround him with threatening looks, but he fearlessly turns
his back on Satan's towers of destruction.

Analysis

In Book V, Eve explains the dream she had during Satan's visit
to her as a toad in Book IV. When Gabriel's angels find Satan "squat
like a toad, close at the ear of Eve," he is attempting by his "devilish
art" to reach "the organs of her fancy" or, in other words, her dreams
(P. L., IV, 800–802). The reader is convinced of his success when
Adam finds her in the morning "with tresses discomposed, and
glowing cheek,/ As through unquiet rest." She relates her disturbing dream to Adam, and it is recognized as a foreshadowing of
Satan's temptation of Eve in Book IX. As is foretold in Eve's dream,
Satan later promises her that she will rise to the stature of a goddess if she eats the fruit of the Tree of Knowledge (P. L., IX, 547).
When she does eat, as is also true in her dream, she experiences a
feeling of "high exaltation" (P. L., IX, 780–94). In both accounts,
Satan, or the Serpent, as he is later portrayed, claims to have eaten
the fruit, boasts of its inward powers, and tempts her to eat too
with the promise that it will produce "strange alteration" in her
degree of reason (P. L., IX, 599–600).

Eve's dream has left her with troubled thoughts, but Adam
comforts her by expounding on the dream psychology of his time.
Though the Freudian theory about dreams and the unconscious
was unheard of in the seventeenth century, Milton's interpretation
of Eve's dream is hauntingly close to Freud's idea of dreams as wish-
fulfillment or "Fancy" that is left unchecked by the waking
consciousness or, as Milton would have it, the faculty of "Reason."

The opening lines of Adam and Eve's morning hymn of praise
to God is closely analogous to Psalms 19:1. "The heavens declare
the glory of God; and the firmament sheweth his handiwork." The
majority of the passage, however, alludes to Psalm 148. Echoes of
the Psalmist pervade their invocation as they call on the planets,
the elements, the trees, the birds of the air, the beasts of the field,
and the angels to join together in praise to the eternal God.

A refrain that reverberates throughout the poetry of *Paradise Lost* is that of free will. Even Satan admits that he has been given the free will to fall (P. L., IV, 66). In speaking to Eve, Adam praises their God who is infinitely good and "As liberal and free as infinite" (P. L., IV, 415). In Book V, Milton has again placed the phrase into the mouth of God himself who declares that he has left Adam and Eve to their "own free will." Raphael has come to warn them about their obedience to their creator but reminds them of their freedom of choice. God has, Raphael says, "ordained thy will/ By nature free."

Led to the bower by Adam, Raphael greets Eve upon arrival with "Hail Mother of Mankind." The poet likens Eve to the Virgin Mary, mother of Jesus, but he also associates her with Venus, goddess of love in Roman mythology, who was awarded a prize for her beauty by Paris on Mount Ida. In referring to Venus as "the fairest goddess," Milton attaches the negative "feigned" to her title. Frank Kermode observes that Milton "is constantly disclaiming these heathen fancies, but is constantly putting them in [his poem]" (Frank Kermode, "Adam Unparadised," p. 135). This is also true in Milton's series of classical comparisons in Book IV as he describes Eden. Though these pagan fields and gardens are beautiful, none can compare to Paradise (P.L., IV, 274). The poet's theme in the opening of his epic is, the poet says, loftier than those of the pagan poets. He announces that he "with no middle flight intends to soar/ Above the Aonian Mount (P. L., I, 14–15). In this way, Milton offers a disclaimer for the use of pagan allusions but, at the same time, enriches his epic by including them.

When Raphael dines with Adam and Eve, he does not merely seem to eat but eats with "real hunger." A parallel to Milton's idea is found in Genesis 18. This is the passage where Abraham entertains three angels, giving them food and drink.

Raphael's account of the "scale of Nature" centers around the idea of a natural order where all things are created in various forms and varying degrees. Created beings become more spiritous and pure as they are proportionately nearer to God. In this hierarchy, God is supreme and all other beings have a natural superior whom they are obligated to obey and a natural inferior whom they must rule. If the hierarchy is broken, disorder and chaos is the result. This happens if an inferior usurps the power of a being that is by nature superior. This idea is central to *Paradise Lost* and to the fall of Man. At this point in the epic, Satan has already attempted to usurp the power of God by claiming equality with him. Satan's fall has created a chain reaction of disorder and chaos which will eventually lead to the fall of Man.

Raphael describes the war in Heaven in a flashback that places the characters before the time of Satan's fall in Book I. This is in keeping with the epic tradition of beginning the poem in *medias res*—in the middle of things. In the poem, God's statement, "This day I have begot whom I declare/ My only Son," is an allusion to the Scriptures. "I will declare the decree; the Lord hath said unto me, Thou art my Son; this day have I begotten thee" (Psalms 2:7). The word "begot" is used in the metaphorical sense rather than the literal. On this particular day, the Son is anointed and proclaimed to be the head of the angels. The angels must hereafter bow to the Son and honor Him as their Lord. Milton did not believe the Son was coeternal with God, but that he was the first thing to be created. It is God's announcement, proclaiming the Son as the angels' superior that causes Satan's jealousy and his consequent rebellion against God. When Satan gathers his troops in the North, he is attempting to flee from God and form a rebellion against him. He argues that paying "knee-tribute" to God was bad enough but to double that honor by bowing to the Son also, cannot be endured. All of his legions of angels agree with him in silent consent except Abdiel. He alone opposes Satan, calling him "blasphemous, false, and proud." He argues that God's law is just, because he is the creator and, therefore, their natural superior. In rebuttal to Abdiel, Satan refutes the idea that God created him, arguing that the angels were "self-begot" and "self-raised." He knows it is a lie and later affirms his true Creator in his soliloquy on Mount Niphates (P. L., IV, 43). Standing firm in spite of opposition, Abdiel is Milton's prototype of those who hold to their convictions against the opinions of the masses.

Study Questions

1. Who is responsible for the evil nature of Eve's dream?
2. What does Eve's dream foreshadow?

3. How does Adam comfort Eve after her frightening dream?

4. Who is asked to join Adam and Eve in their morning praise to God?

5. What kind of food does Eve prepare for Raphael?

6. To whom does Raphael allude when he greets Eve with "Hail Mother of Mankind"?

7. Who has no superior to obey in the "scale of Nature"?

8. Why does Satan rebel against God?

9. Who speaks against Satan when he gathers his legions of angels in the North of Heaven to convince them to rebel against God?

10. How does Satan answer his sole disbeliever's accusation that he is not obeying his creator?

Answers

1. Satan has come to Eve in the form of a toad and has attempted to reach "the organs of her fancy."

2. Eve's dream foreshadows Satan's temptation of Eve and her consequent fall.

3. Adam tells her that evil can come and go in the mind and leave no trace of its presence.

4. Adam and Eve call on the planets, elements, trees, birds, beasts, and angels to join them in their praise of God.

5. Eve prepares the choicest fruits of Paradise for Raphael, their guest.

6. Raphael alludes to Mary, the mother of Jesus. Eve is literally the Mother of Mankind, however.

7. God alone has no superior in the "scale of Nature."

8. Satan is jealous because God has proclaimed the Son as the angels' superior.

9. Abdiel alone speaks against Satan and his rebellion against God.

10. Satan denies that God created him though he knows it is a lie.

Suggested Essay Topics

1. Eve's dream can be seen as a foreshadowing of the fate of mankind. Compare her dream to the temptation and fall in Book IX. What is the symbolism in her temptation to become a goddess. In what way is her flight through the air symbolic of her exalted state of mind after she indulges in the forbidden act? How does she feel about her act of sin when she is awakened by Adam? How does Adam comfort her? Cite examples from the poem to support your argument.

2. Abdiel could be considered a prototype for those who stand alone in their beliefs in the face of a hostile crowd. Compare Abdiel to a person you know in public life. In what way are people like Abdiel an asset to society? Why does no one stand by Abdiel? Do they think he is wrong? Are they afraid of the consequences? Support your argument with examples from the poem.

Book VI

New Characters:

Michael: *leads God's angels in battle in the war in Heaven*

Zophiel: *one of Michael's angels who warns them of the approaching foe, Satan and his legions of angels*

Nisroch: *one of Satan's angels who becomes discouraged with the war*

Summary

Raphael continues his account of Satan's rebellion and the subsequent war in Heaven. Abdiel has flown all night long after leaving Satan and his legions of angels in the North. He arrives in the morning, expecting to warn God's loyal angels of Satan's impending uprising but, to his surprise, finds them in preparation for war. They welcome his return and lead him to the "sacred hill" where God speaks to him from a golden cloud. He commends Abdiel for overcoming Satan's multitudes in the cause of truth, though they have accused him of being perverse. To bear their reproach was far worse than to endure their violence, God says.

God then commands Michael, prince of the celestial armies, and Gabriel, next in rank, to lead their "armed saints" in battle against Satan's "Godless crew." He instructs them to drive the enemy out of Heaven and into their place of punishment, the fiery gulf of Chaos. Among clouds, smoke, and flames, symbols of God's wrath, the ethereal trumpet signals the troops who march forward with a unified purpose. They cross over hills, valleys, and streams and finally see the horizon of the "fiery region" of Satan and his legions in the North. Determined to take over the Mount of God by surprise attack, the powers of Satan are seen advancing toward Michael's troops.

Though it seems incongruous for angel to war against angel, the poet says, the shout of battle is in the air. In the midst of the rush of combat, sits Satan, a parody of the true God on a "gorgeous throne." From his high seat on a "sun-bright chariot," he alights on the ground and advances toward his enemy with "haughty strides." He comes face to face with Abdiel who cannot tolerate Satan's arrogance. Abdiel is surprised to see that the imposter still resembles his former resplendent self. Abdiel calls him a fool for attempting to fight against the omnipotent God who could, with one sweep of the hand, destroy him and submerge his legions of angels into darkness.

Satan accuses Abdiel of arriving before the others so that he can be the first to fight him and, thereby, gain his own personal reward in battle. Denying the omnipotence of God, Satan reminds Abdiel that he and the rest of God's angels prefer sluggish servility to freedom. Abdiel sternly replies that to serve God, who excels "them whom he governs," follows the order of Nature and is, therefore, free. True servitude is to serve an unwise leader who has rebelled against a natural superior. This is true of those who now serve Satan. Abdiel tells Satan that he is not free because he has become a slave to his own image. Challenging Satan to reign in Hell where he will be in chains, Abdiel says that he prefers to serve

in Heaven. Abdiel gives Satan a swift blow on his crest, knocking him back and bringing him to his knees. Satan's legions are stunned. Michael calls for the sound of the trumpet, and the war in Heaven begins. Millions of angels fight as the clashing of spears on armors and the thunderous wheels of the chariots add to the din of battle. The angels, who have the strength to exercise their powers over the elements, fight with "indistinguishable rage." To keep them from destroying Heaven altogether, God steps in to limit their powers.

Throughout the first day of battle, Satan has not met his equal until he encounters Michael who conquers whole squadrons with the sweep of his sword. In an effort to stop him, Satan hastily approaches Michael. Hoping for a truce, Michael stops fighting. He tells Satan that Heaven will not tolerate his rebellion that manifests itself in violence and war. He and his "wicked crew" will be driven out of Heaven "to the place of evil, Hell." Satan challenges Michael's "airy threats" stating that Michael cannot back them up with deeds. The two come face to face, fighting with such "godlike power" that the rest of the angels stop their combat and step back in expectant horror. These leaders wave their fiery swords in the air and make horrid circles. Michael's sword is so sharp that it completely shears Satan's right side. For the first time, Satan feels pain, but his body is made of "ethereal substance," and it quickly heals. "Nectarous humor" flows from his wound, however, leaving stains on his armor. His angels come from all sides to carry him back to his chariot. His confidence has been shaken, and his pride has been hurt, but his body soon heals because spirits cannot die. They can, the poet says, mend themselves and assume the color, shape, or size that they like best.

Meanwhile, the war continues and Gabriel wounds Moloch who runs away in pain. Thousands of Satan's angels are wounded that day, but not all of God's heroes will be named, the poet says, for angels in Heaven do not seek the praise of men.

The saints, by contrast, stand invulnerable and impenetrable, appearing sinless and obedient to God. They are not weary from battle nor are they in pain. Night falls, and a truce is declared as Michael and his troops set up camp with guards watching the fires. Satan's crew does not sleep but is called to council to discuss their strategies for the next day of battle. Satan suggests that the remedy for their failures might be more violent weapons. Nisroch speaks up, complaining that the sides have been unequal since Michael's angels cannot feel the pain that Satan's army can. He endorses Satan's idea of more forcible weapons, calling for someone who can invent them. With assurance, Satan replies that they have already been invented. He describes them as "hollow engines long and round" or, in other words, cannons that are "thick-rammed" with a "touch of fire" or gunpowder. Encouraged by their hopeful prospects, Satan's angels go straight to work, digging up the "celestial soil" to mine the natural elements for their engines and ammunition.

In the morning, Michael's victorious angels look around for the enemy. Zophiel is the first to see them and calls out a warning. In readiness, they meet Satan's squadrons who carefully hide their "devilish enginry." When the two sides finally confront each other, Satan tricks his enemies into believing they have come in peace. He orders his angels to step aside to reveal the "deep-throated engines." The cannon is then fired and thousands of Michael's angels are knocked down. Satan and Belial jeer derisively at their enemies' plight, but Michael's angels soon respond by discarding their weapons and picking up entire hills to throw at Satan's cannons. They bury the cannons under the "weight of mountains," and then attack Satan's troops, burying whole legions of angels who moan in pain.

Looking down from his "sanctuary of Heaven," God decides to intervene by sending the Son to drive Satan and his followers out of Heaven and into the "utter deep." The war has lasted for two days and no solution has been found, God says. Since both sides were created equal, the battle will go on perpetually unless it is stopped.

The Son, honored by God's request, agrees to end the war in Heaven. On the third day, he leaves his seat at God's right hand to mount the heavenly chariot that is escorted by four "cherubic shapes." Victory rides at his right hand, surrounded with smoke and flames and is attended by 10,000 angels and 20,000 "chariots of God."

When he sees the sign of "Messiah" overhead, Michael divides his army to make a path for the Son to pass through. The Son commands the "uprooted hills" to go back to their rightful places and they obey. Satan's troops see the Son advancing as they rally their powers and harden their sensibilities. Vowing that they will either win the fight against God and Messiah or fall into ruin, they prepare for their final battle. The Son calls to Michael's angels, telling them he will now fight the enemy alone. Changing his countenance to that of terror, the Son, full of wrath, rides his chariot among Satan's troops and throws 10,000 thunders at them. In astonishment and fear, they drop their armor as they are driven to the wall of Heaven that opens wide and rolls inward, disclosing a "spacious gap" into the deep. To escape the Son's wrath, they throw themselves into the "bottomless pit" where they fall for nine days. "Disburdened Heaven" rejoices over the victory of Messiah whose triumph is celebrated as he returns to his Father's throne.

Raphael ends his account by warning Adam that Satan is now plotting to seduce the earthly pair into disobedience to God. He tells him not to listen to Satan's temptations and to warn Eve to do the same. He hopes that Adam has learned, "by terrible example," the consequence of disobedience to God.

Analysis

In the opening of Book VI, Abdiel appears before God after his long flight from the North. He has stood alone against Satan's evil angels and remained faithful to God. God commends him with "Servant of God, well done, well hast thou fought/ The better fight." These words are an allusion to the parable of the talents. "Well done, good and faithful servant" (Matt. 25:23). God's approval is reward enough for Abdiel.

The account of the war in Heaven is essential to a fuller understanding of Books I and II where our sympathies often tend to lean to the side of Satan and his followers. Raphael's description of the war in Book VI clarifies Satan's evil nature and further delineates Milton's purpose in the epic which is to "justify the ways of God to men" (P. L., I, 26).

In his exchange with Abdiel, Satan gives lip service to his own cause of liberty, but his actions prove him false and proud. He is an opportunist who wishes to usurp the power and position of God, and his jealousy of the Son is caused by his own self interests. In the war, "servility with freedom" will contend, Satan says. He pictures himself on the side of freedom, but Abdiel sees through his façade when he perceptively exposes Satan's deceit. "Thyself not free, but to thyself enthralled." Though he wishes to be free of servitude, ironically, he does not believe in equality. In an earlier speech to his followers, he has already affirmed this belief. "If not equal all, yet free,/ Equally free; for orders and degrees/ Jar not with liberty" (P. L., V, 791–93). Abdiel forecasts Satan's eventual doom. "Reign thou in Hell thy kingdom, let me serve/ In Heaven." Abdiel's prediction comes true, and when Satan arrives in Hell, he has not changed, still believing it is "better to reign in Hell than serve in Heaven" (P. L., I, 272).

It is a generally accepted view that Milton's authority for the war in Heaven is Revelation 12. This source gave him the names of the opposing leaders. "And there was war in heaven; Michael and his angels fought against the dragon (Satan); and the dragon fought and his angels (12:7). It also gave him the reference to Satan's fall. "And the great dragon was cast out, that old serpent, called the Devil, and Satan . . . and his angels were cast out with him" (12:9). It is believed that the "third part of the stars of heaven" (12:4) refers to the size of Satan's army that fell with him. There are also examples of metaphorical references to the "armor of God" (Eph. 6:11, 14, 16, 17), but the Bible gives little detailed information about the war in heaven. It is believed that Milton turned mostly to the epics of Homer and Virgil for skillful descriptions of warfare. The gods in Homer's *Iliad*, for example, could have been his model for the legions of angels who wield larger-than-life weapons, resulting in unimaginable ruin. By patterning his battle scenes after those of the classical poets, Milton was fulfilling the standard of the true epic.

In the war in Heaven, shame and ridicule are far more disturbing to its victims than the actual violence of the war. God himself sets the tone for this attitude when he tells Abdiel that "Universal reproach" is "far worse to bear/ Than violence." When Michael's sword shears Satan's right side, he is soon healed, but he continues to suffer from the shameful experience.

> Gnashing for anguish and despite and shame
> To find himself not matchless, and his pride
> Humbled by such rebuke, so far beneath
> His confidence to equal God in power.

Moloch too has "fled bellowing" when he is stabbed by Gabriel. The implication can be seen in the tone which is one of insult more than injury.

Even Michael's angels become victims of derision when they are knocked down by the newly invented cannon balls of Satan's troops. Until this point, they have been the victors in the strife, but now they are concerned about saving face.

> What should they do? If on they rushed, repulse
> Repeated, and indecent overthrow
> Doubled, would render them yet more despised,
> And to their foes a laughter.

It is obvious that fear does not even enter into the situation. Satan is quick to notice "their plight" and immediately capitalizes on his advantage over them. Addressing Belial, but making sure the enemy hears, Satan derides the proud victors for their hesitation to advance in the battle. Scoffing at them, he pretends to be puzzled about their retreat. Belial enters into Satan's game, mocking his distraught enemies with a play on words. "The terms we sent were terms of weight,/ Of hard contents."

The scene reaches the height of all absurdity, however, when, out of rage, Michael's angels discard their weapons and begin to uproot mountains, throwing them at the cannons and burying them. The battle becomes a laughable farce as whole mountains meet other mountains in midair. Entire armies are buried, but they continue to fight underground. God finally decides to stop them. Even when the Son comes to drive them out of Heaven, Satan and his legions cannot suffer the shame of defeat. They decide to stand proudly against the Son and risk their fall, rather than subject themselves to ridicule.

Satan's invention of the "hollow engines" that bore a "touch of fire" alludes to the use of cannons and gunpowder. The English

Gunpowder Plot of 1605 was originated by Guy Fawkes in an effort to blow up the Houses of Parliament when King James I was present. Gunpowder had long been considered an invention of the devil, and the idea was still prevalent in Milton's day. For his description of gunpowder, he is indebted to the earlier Rennaisance poets. Spenser, in *The Faerie Queene*, also sees it as a creation of the devil.

> As when that diuelish yron Engin wrought
> In deepest Hell, and framd by Furies skill,
> With windy Nitre and quick Sulphur fraught,
> And ramd with bullet round, ordained to kill.
>
> (Edmund Spenser, *The Faerie Queene*, I, 7,13)

Unlike Spenser, Milton attributed the origin of gunpowder to Heaven rather than Hell.

The war in Heaven is a struggle between good and evil and does not end until God intervenes. It is a "perpetual fight" that is "endless" with "no solution" until the Messiah comes to drive the evil ones out of Heaven. Helen Gardner compares "the expulsion of Satan and his followers from Heaven" to Michelangelo's *Last Judgement* where Christ casts down his enemies on the day of judgement (Helen Gardner, "The Cosmic Theme," 67). It is only then that good will overcome evil.

Raphael warns Adam about the "reward of disobedience" at the end of Book VI; this is why he has gone to such great lengths to describe the war in Heaven. In comparing "things in Heaven" to "things on Earth," Adam has, by example, been forewarned about the temptations of Satan and the punishment for disobedience. For the first time, Adam is made aware that Satan is now "plotting how he may seduce/ Thee also from obedience." He reminds Adam to caution Eve about Satan's presence in Eden.

Study Questions

1. Who commends Abdiel for opposing Satan and his legions of angels?

2. What is Abdiel's definition of servitude?

3. Who is the leader of God's angels in the war in Heaven?

4. Which side uses gunpowder in the war in Heaven?

5. Which side picks up mountains and uses them as weapons?

6. Why does neither of the armies win the war?

7. Who is sent to end the war and drive Satan and his angels out of Heaven?

8. For how many days do Satan and his angels fall?

9. Who is the narrator for the story of the war in Heaven?

10. What does the narrator warn Adam about?

Answers

1. God commends Abdiel for speaking against Satan and bearing the reproach of the multitudes.

2. Abdiel tells Satan that servitude is to serve an unwise leader (namely Satan) who has rebelled against a natural superior.

3. Michael is the leader of God's angels in the war.

4. Satan's troops use gunpowder against the angels who have been victorious up to that point.

5. Michael's angels pick up mountains and throw them at their opponents.

6. Both armies were created equal and cannot win. The war would have gone on indefinitely if God had not intervened.

7. God sends the Son to end the war and drive Satan and his angels out of Heaven.

8. Satan and his angels fall for nine days.

9. Raphael narrates the story of the war in Heaven.

10. Raphael warns Adam that Satan is in Eden, plotting their fall.

Suggested Essay Topics

1. Satan proposes the idea of freedom in Book VI. Discuss the reason why he does not live up to his noble idea. Does he think freedom and equality should be given to everyone? Whose power does he intend to usurp in the name of free-

dom? Why does Abdiel accuse him of lacking freedom? Cite examples from the poem to prove your point.

2. In the war in Heaven, the angels are unduly concerned with the ridicule of the opposing army. Discuss this idea in relationship to the human race. Was Milton touching on a human reality? Is "universal reproach" harder to bear than "violence"? Give examples from the poem to support your opinion.

Book VII

Summary

The poet invokes the muse, Urania, but he makes it clear that it is "the meaning, not the name" that he is calling forth. His muse is not one of the nine sisters who was born on Mount Olympus but is "heavenly born" instead. Wisdom is her sister and the two played in the presence of the "Almighty Father" before the hills were created. The poet asks the muse to guide him safely down to Earth, his native element, from his wanderings in Heaven. His poem is only half sung, but he now feels safer and more familiar with mortal things on Earth despite the danger and "evil days" that have come upon him. He asks the muse to find an audience for his words and to drive away "Bacchus" and his "revellers" who threaten him with their "barbarous dissonance" and their drunken violence.

Raphael has already warned Adam and Eve, with the example of Satan's fall, that they are subject to the same fate in Paradise if they disobey God's commands. Since Raphael has described the war in Heaven for their instruction, Adam now asks him to impart further knowledge about how the world was created and for what purpose. He has the desire to know so that he can glorify God for all his works. They have time, Adam says, since Night has not yet fallen, or, if need be, they could delay the coming of Night to allow time for the story. Raphael replies that he has been instructed by God to give "knowledge within bounds." Knowledge is like food that is to be absorbed with temperance, or it will soon turn "wisdom to folly."

Raphael begins by explaining that the expulsion of Satan and the angels has "dispeopled Heaven." To repair the loss, God decides to create another world with a new race of men who would, "by degrees of merit," raise themselves to the level of Heaven into one happy kingdom without end. God appoints the Son to perform the creation of the world and set the boundaries of Heaven and Earth.

The angels rejoice in adoration of God for creating good out of evil by bringing a new race into their "vacant room" in Heaven. The Son, crowned with the radiance of the Father, leaves on his chariot to create the world. As he approaches, the gates of Heaven open wide to let the King of Glory pass through. The Son stands on the edge of the "heavenly ground" as he views the vast Abyss that appears "as a sea, dark, wasteful," and "wild." Chaos hears him call out, to silence the "troubled waves." He then uses God's golden compasses to circumscribe the Universe and form Heaven and Earth. The Spirit of God spreads his wings over the water, instilling it with warmth. He solidifies the elements and shapes them into the form of a globe.

God calls forth the light and it appears in a "radiant cloud," for the sun has not been created yet. He then divides the light and calls it Day and the darkness is called Night. The celestial choirs joyously sing praises for the first day of creation.

On the second day, God creates the firmament "amid the waters," far removed from Chaos so there will be nothing to disturb its form. He names the firmament Heaven, and the heavenly angels again sing joyously.

God gathers the waters together that appear "over all the face of Earth" and, on the third day, orders dry land to appear. Mountains rise and rivers are channeled into the seas, and God knows that it is good. He then calls for the Earth to cover its barren fields and put forth tender grass, fruit trees, flowering plants, clustering vines, shrubs, and bushes. A "dewy mist" rises to water the plants, and Earth now seems like Heaven where the "gods might dwell."

On the fourth day, God creates the planets, the stars, the moon, and the sun that direct the days, the years, and the seasons. He then calls on the waters to generate the reptiles, the "great whales," and the fish and creates the birds that fly in the air which solemnizes the fifth day of creation.

On the last day of creation, the sixth, God orders the Earth to bring forth the beasts. Earth opens "her fertile womb" and living creatures rise up out of the ground, either solitary, in pairs, or in herds, and shake the dirt off their backs. Insects, worms, snakes, and numberless creatures that crawl on the ground are then created.

The "master work," above the brute and endowed with reason, has not yet appeared. God speaks to the Son, telling him he should now create Man in their image. The Son forms Adam out of the dust of the ground and breathes the breathe of life into his nostrils, and he becomes a living soul. He creates Adam as a male and his consort, Eve, as a female, telling them to be fruitful and multiply. He gives them dominion over all living creatures and allows them to taste all the pleasant fruits of the garden except one: the fruit of the Tree of Knowledge of good and evil.

When the Creator is finished at the end of the sixth day, he looks at all he has made and says it is "entirely good." He returns to Heaven where he is welcomed at the "everlasting gates" with the symphonious music of 10,000 angelic harps.

On the seventh day, the Son sits down with his Father and rests from his labors as he blesses and hallows the Sabbath. The day is spent resting from work and singing halleluiahs in celebration of God's new creation. Raphael has now filled Adam's request to describe the creation of the world and asks whether he has any other questions that stay within the bounds of human understanding.

Analysis

In the opening lines of Book VII, the poet invokes the muse, Urania, the classical muse of astronomy. She was one of the nine daughters of Zeus and Mnemosyne, goddess of memory. As attendants of Apollo, the god of poetry, the muses were routinely called on by poets before they began to write. The Christian poets often referred to Urania as "the heavenly" and called on her for divine inspiration. In his reference to Urania, the poet names her but is quick to qualify his allusion to her by associating her in "meaning" only with the muse that is "heavenly born." His muse's sister is named Wisdom, and the two siblings have played together in the presence of God before the hills were formed. This alludes to Prov-

erbs 8:29–30. "When he appointed the foundations of the earth: Then I (Wisdom) was with him, as one brought up with him." In this way Milton associates his muse with the Holy Spirit, the muse of Moses, but enriches the epic with the traditions of the classics. This is also reminiscent of his invocation to the "Heavenly Muse" in Book I where he calls on the muse who inspired Moses on Mount Sinai (Exod. 19:20).

In Book VII the poet has left the war in Heaven and will now stand on Earth where he feels safer using his own "mortal voice" though he has "fallen on evil days." Many commentators believe that the "evil days" are a reference to the time after the Restoration of Charles II when Milton was in grave danger. He had supported the execution of Charles I in his *Tenure of Kings and Magistrates* and championed the Puritan cause as Latin Secretary under Oliver Cromwell. He was arrested for his political crimes but was eventually released.

The poet continues by comparing his own fate to that of Orpheus, the Thracian bard, who was torn limb from limb by the crowd when he would not join their frenzied celebration of Bacchus. The muse is Calliope, one of the nine, who could not save him though she was his mother. Milton sees himself as Orpheus, a poet living in an antagonistic society. The "barbarous dissonance" is a reference to the unruly crowds in London after the Restoration. Milton also uses the myth of Orpheus in "Lycidas" (57–63) to question his own high artistic standards that are not appreciated by his contemporaries.

In Book VII we realize that Adam's curiosity has not been satisfied by Raphael's account of the war in Heaven. He has a further "desire to know" what transpired when the World began, and he asks Raphael to tell him about the creation of Eden "before his memory." He craves this knowledge just as one would crave water.

> as one whose drouth
> Yet scarce allayed still eyes the current stream,
> Whose liquid murmur heard new thirst excites.

His desire for knowledge is artistically woven through the passage with metaphors of thirst. "Drouth, stream, liquid murmur, and thirst are expressive of Adam's longing to know. He quickly checks his longing, however, claiming he has no intention of going beyond God's limits of forbidden knowledge. "If unforbid thou mayst unfold/ What we, not to explore the secrets ask/ Of his eternal empire." Raphael answers him with still another metaphor, equating knowledge to food that "needs no less her temperance over appetite." The archangel has been instructed by God to answer Adam's questions "within bounds." Excessive knowledge, Raphael says, will turn "Wisdom to folly."

As the Son approaches the gates of Heaven, he hears the "harmonious sound" and sees the "golden hinges moving" to allow the "King of Glory" to pass. He then goes forth into Chaos to create the World. This is reminiscent of Satan who also goes forth into Chaos in Book II, but, in contrast to the Son, Satan seeks revenge by corrupting God's creation. The gates of Hell contrast sharply with the gates of Heaven. With a "jarring sound . . . their hinges grate/ Harsh thunder" (P. L., II, 881–82) as they are unlocked to let Satan pass through.

The Son's first act of creation is to silence the troubled waves and pronounce peace upon the Deep. The allusion is to the words of Jesus of Galilee. "And he arose, and rebuked the wind, and said unto the sea, Peace be still. And the wind ceased, and there was a great calm" (Mark 4:39). Milton portrays the Son with the same divine power that he demonstrates as the Son of Man on Earth.

The Scriptures also lend authority to Milton's image of the "golden compasses" by which the Son circumscribes a section of Chaos for the creation of Heaven and Earth. "When he prepared the heavens, I was there: when he set a compass upon the face of the depth" (Prov. 8:27).

The creation of the leviathon, "hugest of living creatures," is reminiscent of the leviathon that is analogous to the size of Satan who is chained on the burning lake in Book I (P. L., I, 201). Milton's source was the Bible (Job 41:1). It is often thought that the leviathon in the Bible is a whale, but Milton makes a distinction between the two by also creating a whale.

As Raphael ends his story, the angels are glorifying the Son on the Sabbath day with songs of praise for his act of creation. They tell the Son that "to create/ Is greater than created to destroy." They feel he is more noble now that he returns from his act of creation

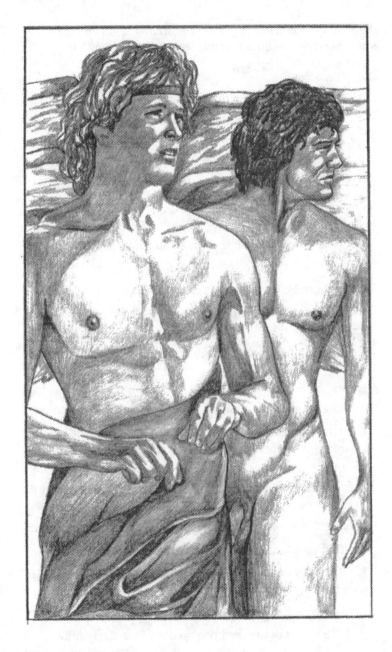

than he was when he returned from driving Satan and his angels out of Heaven. "To create" is greater than "to destroy."

Study Questions

1. What is the name of the poet's muse?

2. What does the poet mean when he says that it is the meaning, not the name of the muse that he is calling forth?

3. What does God plan to do to repair the loss of Satan and his angels in Heaven?

4. Who is appointed by God to perform the act of creation?

5. Had the light appeared before the sun?

6. When is the firmament created and what is it later called?

7. On which day of creation does dry land appear?

8. Besides Man, what else is created on the sixth day?

9. What do God, the Son, and the angels in Heaven do on the Sabbath?

10. What happens when the Son reaches the gates of Heaven?

Answers

1. The poet's muse is named Urania, the muse of astronomy.

2. The poet associates the meaning of the muse with the God of the Scriptures but names Urania from classical mythology.

3. God plans to create a new race called Man to eventually fill the vacancy in Heaven.

4. The Son is appointed to create the universe.

5. God calls forth the light before the sun is created.

6. The firmament is created on the second day, and it is called Heaven.

7. Dry land appears on the third day.

8. The beasts of the field rise up out of the dust on the sixth day. Insects, worms, snakes, and other numberless creatures also appear.

9. God, the Son, and the angels rest and sing praises on the Sabbath.

10. The Son hears harmonious music and sees the golden hinges as the gates of Heaven open to let him pass through.

Suggested Essay Topics

1. When the Son reaches the gates of Heaven, he hears melodious music and sees the beauty of its "golden hinges." Contrast this image to that of the gates of Hell in Book II. Explain the symbolism inherent in these images. What does the music symbolize? What do the golden hinges symbolize? In what way are the grating hinges of the gates of Hell symbolic of Satan's fall? Cite examples from the poem to support your answer.

2. Milton describes Adam's craving for knowledge with the metaphors of thirst and hunger. Explain these metaphors. How do they relate to knowledge? How is temperence associated with the acquisition of knowledge? What is the difference between wisdom and folly in relation to knowledge? Support your answer with the use of examples from the poem.

Book VIII

Summary

Adam has been so captivated by Raphael's discourse on the creation of the World that he waits expectantly for him to continue. When he realizes that Raphael has finished, he thanks him appropriately. His thirst for knowledge has been allayed, Adam says, but yet another doubt remains that can only be resolved by the archangel. Adam is troubled by the disproportions in Nature in which a superfluous number of celestial bodies revolve around the "sedentary Earth" that is merely a spot or atom compared to the firmament.

When Eve sees that Adam is entering into an intellectual conversation with Raphael, she excuses herself to attend to her garden.

She would be delighted by such conversation and is capable of understanding it, but she prefers to hear it from Adam who will mix his explanations with interesting digressions and "conjugal caresses."

Raphael tells Adam he does not blame him for being curious, but it is not important for him to know whether the celestial bodies revolve around the Earth or whether it is the Earth that moves. Heaven is likened to the Book of God where Adam can learn the seasons, hours, days, months, and years. God conceals the rest of his secrets from Man and is probably laughing at the "quaint opinions" of those who conjecture about the movements of the planets in the universe. It is not "great or bright" that determines excellence, Raphael says, since the "bright luminaries" shine for Man's benefit and could not fulfill their purpose without him. The spaciousness of the entire universe is too large for Man so the rest is ordained for the use of the omnipotent God. Raphael goes on to say that there is no advantage for Man to go beyond the limits of his knowledge. He instructs Adam to concern himself only with his life and that of his "fair Eve" and leave other worlds to "God above." Adam is satisfied with Raphael's explanation and relieved to know he has been "taught to live/ The easiest way." The "prime wisdom" is to learn of ordinary things in one's own "daily life," Adam says.

Conversing with Raphael seems like Heaven to Adam, and he offers to tell the story of his own creation in order to detain Raphael further. Raphael is pleased to listen to Adam's account since on the day of creation the archangel had been on an excursion to the gates of Hell to prevent a spy from escaping while God was performing his work. To their relief the gates were locked, but inside they heard tormented cries from the fallen angels in Hell, and they gladly returned to Heaven before the coming of the Sabbath.

Adam then describes with difficulty how human life began. As he awakes from sleep, he finds himself lying in a "balmy sweat" on a soft bed of "flowery herbs." The sun soon dries him as he gazes up at Heaven. Instinctively, he springs to his feet, surveying the landscape and all living creatures. With joy in his heart, he then peruses his own body, trying to establish his identity and the reason for his existence. He finds his voice and asks the sun and hills and all living creatures how he has come to this place. By his own instincts he knows he was created by "some great Maker" and asks where he might find him but receives no answer. Pensively, he sits down on a bank of flowers and falls asleep. God comes to him in a dream, leading him to the "garden of bliss." When he awakes, he falls at the feet of God in adoration. Lifting him up, God tells Adam he has found the one he was seeking. He presents Adam with the gift of Paradise where he may "eat freely" all fruits except one: the fruit from the "Tree of Knowledge of good and ill" growing next to the "Tree of Life" in Paradise. The penalty of disobedience, God says, is death and the loss of his immortal state. God's interdiction still rings in his ear, Adam says, though the choice is his to make.

God presents the entire Earth as a gift to Adam and his descendants, promising them dominion over all the animals. As a sign of his power over the birds and beasts, Adam is allowed to name them. Addressing the "Heavenly Vision," Adam admonishes him for creating Man in solitude when all the animals are in pairs. God replies that Adam is not alone since he has jurisdiction over all living creatures and can order them to entertain him at any time. Careful not to offend, Adam implores God to grant him the fellowship of one with whom he can share "rational delight," a human consort.

Though God is "not displeased," he reminds Adam that he, the Creator, is alone too and can only converse with the creatures he has made. These are all his inferiors just as Adam's animals are beneath him in rank. In lowliness Adam replies that God is already perfect and Man is not. Adam must complete his imperfection with a human companion with whom he can then propagate the race.

Thus far Adam has been put to the test several times, and God has been pleased each time. Even before Adam spoke, God says, he knew it was not good for "Man to be alone." God then causes Adam to fall asleep but leaves his "cell/ Of fancy" open. Adam, thinking he is in a trance, sees a Shape (God) opening his left side to extract one of his ribs. He forms the rib into a creature whose name is Woman. She looks at Adam and turns away, completely disappearing in the dark. Waking from his dream, he becomes desperate to find her and vows he will follow her and beg her to stay. Meanwhile, the voice of her "Heavenly Maker" has been guiding her to Adam. They meet and Adam leads her to the nuptial bower as all created nature around them rejoices in celebration of the happy occasion.

Adam's passion for Eve leaves him weak, he says. He feels that Nature has failed him since he lacks the strength to resist Eve's beauty. Though Eve should, by nature, be his inferior, when he approaches "her loveliness" she is "in herself complete." Whatever she "wills to do or say/ Seems wisest" when Adam is in her presence. Raphael rebukes Adam sharply with "contracted brow," telling him that Wisdom will not desert him in this matter. He should love Eve, Raphael says, but not hold himself in "subjection" to her. If he demonstrates self-esteem, "she will acknowledge" him as "her head." Raphael admonishes Adam to control his passion with reason. If he would strive to rise above the animals, he must substitute "carnal pleasure" with "heavenly love."

Half abashed by Raphael's words, Adam replies that nothing delights him more than the "thousand decencies that daily flow/ From all her (Eve's) words and actions." He then asks Raphael how the heavenly spirits express love to each other. Blushing, the archangel replies that spirits are happy and "if spirits embrace/ Total they mix, union of pure with pure."

It is time to part, Raphael says, as he leaves with the warning to Adam to "take heed lest passion sway/ Thy judgment," though he has been given the freedom to "stand fast" or fall. Following Raphael with a benediction, Adam invites him to return often. Raphael ascends into Heaven, and Adam retreats to his earthly bower.

Analysis

The belief in the plurality of habitable worlds has already been alluded to at the end of Book VII (620–22). In Book VIII Raphael moves into a full-scale discourse on astronomy, a frequent subject of debate in the seventeenth century. Copernicus had argued, in the sixteenth century, that the Earth and all planets in our solar system move around the sun. This replaced the Ptolemaic idea, formulated 1,400 years earlier, that the Earth is at the center of the universe in a motionless state. In the Copernican system the moon and the planets were thought to be like the Earth. Raphael asserts reasonably that "if land be there" the planets could also have "fields and inhabitants." Milton reflects the seventeenth-century arguments for and against the Ptolemaic system through Raphael's words. It does not matter, Raphael says, whether "the sun predominant in

Heaven/ Rise on the Earth, or Earth rise on the sun." Adam should concern himself only with things that lie before him in "daily life."

Thus far, Adam's requests to Raphael for information (about the war in Heaven and the creation of the world) have stayed within the proper limits for Man, but he now demonstrates a boldness we have not seen before. As if to test Raphael to see how far he can go, Adam questions the disproportions in God's divine creation.

> reasoning I oft admire
> How Nature wise and frugal could commit
> Such disproportions, with superfluous hand
> So many nobler bodies to create,
> Greater so manifold, to this one use (to officiate light).

Raphael rebukes Adam by telling him to "be lowly wise" and not worry about "things too high." The point Raphael is making is not only that information about other worlds are God's concern, but also that Adam has overstepped his human bounds which is a potential danger for him. Adam's thirst for knowledge has reached limits beyond his place on the scale of nature, and he is now questioning God's wisdom in creating a superfluous solar system that he thinks is disproportionately large for its small task of "officiating light" for the Earth. Ogden sees Adam's change of attitude in this case as a "spiritual error" that prepares us "for further revelations of his weakness" such as "his potentially inordinate love of Eve" (H. V. S. Ogden, "The Crisis of Paradise Lost Reconsidered," 321). Adam describes Eve as a woman who has completely enchanted him.

> that what she wills to do or say
> Seems wisest, virtuousest, discreetest, best;
> All higher knowledge in her presence falls
> Degraded. Wisdom in discourse with her
> Loses discountenanced, and like Folly shows.

Raphael rebukes Adam for exalting Eve above her position in the scale of nature. Adam allows her to rule him and, thereby, upsets the natural order. Book VIII foreshadows Adam's passion that rules his reason and ultimately leads to his fall in Book IX.

Raphael has captivated Adam's interest in the accounts of the war in Heaven and the creation of the world. Adam now wishes to reciprocate by telling the archangel his story about "how human life began." Raphael would gladly listen to Adam's account, he says, since he had been on a mission that day to guard the gates of Hell and keep the world safe for God's act of creation. It is hard, Adam says, to tell how his life began, "for who himself beginning knew?" This is reminiscent of Satan's words to Abdiel in Book V. "We knew no time when we were not as now" (859). There is a striking dissimilarity between the tone of Satan's words and that of Adam's, however. Since he cannot remember the day the Maker gave him being, Satan argues that he must be "self-begot" and denies that God created him. In contrast, Adam immediately recognizes that he has come "not of myself; by some great Maker then." He calls out to all of Nature to tell him where he might find his Maker so that he can adore him.

Adam describes his first moments as a sound sleep from which he awakes, met by the drying rays of the sun. "In balmy sweat," which with his beams the sun/ Soon dried, and on the reeking moisture fed." This is reminiscent of an earlier passage where Raphael justifies Adam's concern about the disproportionate number of heavenly bodies by explaining that "those bright luminaries/ Officious, but to thee, Earth's habitant." The sun warms him but its rays also feed on Adam's moisture which gives credence to Raphael's earlier assertion that "the sun that barren shines . . . on itself works no effect" (94–5). Geoffrey Hartman suggests that the image of Adam waking to the sun is "an entirely unhurtful, sympathetic, even symbiotic relation: what one creature takes from another benefits both (Hartman, "Adam on the Grass with Balsamum," 221). Adam needs the sun's warmth and the sun feeds on his moisture. The language supports their reciprocal state of being in its comparable alliterative phrases—"balmy sweat" and "beams the sun" are artfully placed in juxtaposition. It is the sun that Adam first names, personifying it as "fair light." He also calls on the "enlightened Earth" and all the "fair creatures" who "live and move." Adam's first hours are happy ones, depicted with bright images of light and fairness, but he becomes pensive when he cannot find his creator. This alludes to the words of Job who says, "Oh that I knew where I might find him!" (Job 23:3).

In presenting Paradise to Adam, God gives him dominion over the birds and beasts, asking him to name them according to their kind. Adam names them and as the animals approach him two by two, he notices that God has provided amply "but with me/ I see not who partakes." Adam complains to God that there can be no happiness in solitude. Patrides sees this incident as the "first instance of man's free will in action" (C. A. Patrides, "Because We Freely Love," 120). Free will is a theme that runs throughout Milton's epic and, in this case, Adam's complaint meets with God's approval.

As Adam finishes his account of the creation of Man and Woman, the talk about his feeling for Eve leads him to ask Raphael how angels express their love for each other. Raphael blushes but tells Adam it is sufficient to know angels are happy and without love there would be no happiness. In parting, Raphael again warns Adam not to let his passion sway his judgment.

Study Questions

1. What is Raphael's answer to Adam's question about the superfluous number of celestial bodies that serve only Earth?

2. What does Adam think is the primary purpose of the celestial bodies?

3. What does Adam see in his first moments of life?

4. Why are Adam and the sun important to each other?

5. What is the first thing that Adam wants to find after his creation?

6. What is an example of free will in Book VIII?

7. How did God create Eve?

8. What happens to Adam when he observes Eve's loveliness?

9. What warning does Raphael give Adam about his wisdom concerning Eve?

10. What is Raphael's last warning to Adam before he goes back to Heaven?

Answers

1. Raphael tells Adam to concern himself only with his life and leave other worlds to God.

2. Adam thinks the primary purpose of the celestial bodies is "to officiate light."

3. Adam sees the sun that is drying his "balmy sweat."

4. Adam needs the sun for warmth just as the sun needs Adam to fulfill its purpose.

5. The first thing Adam wants to find is his creator.

6. Free will is seen in Adam's complaint about his own solitude.

7. Eve was formed from one of Adam's ribs.

8. Adam's passion takes over his reason when Eve appears.

9. Raphael tells Adam he should love Eve but not hold himself in subjection to her.

10. Raphael's last warning to Adam is to "take heed lest passion sway/ Thy judgment."

Suggested Essay Topics

1. Adam and the sun have somewhat of a symbiotic relationship. Describe their mutual give and take in the first moments of Adam's life. What does the sun do for Adam? What does Adam provide for the sun? Why does he personify the sun and call on him before the other elements of nature? Give examples from the poem to support your argument.

2. Milton implies that Adam's passion for Eve has led him to exalt her above her position in the scale of nature. Apply this seventeenth-century idea to our modern-day society. Is man representative of reason? Is woman symbolic of passion? To support your idea use examples from the poem.

Book IX

Summary

The poet must now dispense with all the talk about God or angel as the guests of Man in Paradise, he says. He can no longer indulge them in food and conversation but must now change the epic to a tragic tone. Man will disobey God, and Heaven will rebuke Man, judging him for bringing Sin, Death, and Misery into the World. Though it is a "sad task," it has a more heroic theme than those of prior epics dealing with the wrath of Achilles (the *Iliad*), the anger of Neptune against Odysseus (the *Odyssey*), and Juno's hostility toward Aeneas, Cytherea's son (the *Aeneid*), along with the anger of Turnus for the loss of Lavinia in the same epic. He hopes to obtain a style equal to the dignity of his theme from the inspiration of his heavenly muse who visits him nightly. The subject for his epic, Milton says, was chosen long ago, but he began composing it much later. It is not his nature to write about wars, the only theme that has been regarded as worthy for the heroic epic. He feels the same way about detailed accounts of "gorgeous knights" in jousting tournaments that are "long and tedious" while their true "heroic martyrdom" is left unsung. He is confident that his higher theme will be sufficient to raise his epic poem to the heroic level unless people in his historical period do not accept his poem. The cold climate, thought to be unfavorable to the mind, or his old age might keep him from finishing his intended work, but he looks to his muse to continue her nightly visits and prevent these things from happening.

Satan, who had been driven from Eden by Gabriel, returns eight days later and enters Paradise through an underground channel of the Tigris River. Rising up through a fountain, Satan finds himself next to the Tree of Life. Afraid of being caught under the watchful eye of Uriel, angel of the sun, he has fled for seven continual nights, always careful to keep himself within the shadow of the Earth. He has searched the Earth for a creature that would be a "fit vessel" for his fraudulent temptation of Adam and Eve and finally decides that he will enter the body of a serpent who would subtly hide his "diabolic power."

Before he disguises himself as the serpent, Satan, overcome with "inward grief," speaks to the Earth with "bursting passion," mourning his lost state in Heaven. The Earth is like Heaven, if not better, Satan says, for God built it second, "reforming what was old!" Satan sees the Earth at the center of the universe with all the "officious lamps" shining for its benefit. The light of the sun and stars produces plants and animals all the way up the scale of nature to Man. It would be delightful to walk the Earth, he says. He regrets that he cannot find refuge in the pleasures of Paradise and is tormented by its contrast to his own existence. He suddenly remembers, however, that he does not wish to dwell in Heaven nor on Earth unless he can reign over the supreme God. He can, in fact, only find peace by destroying, and it is Man he intends to destroy.

For marring in one day what it took God six days to create, Satan will be given the sole glory among his "infernal Powers" in Hell. He feels it was out of God's spite to the fallen angels that he later created Man to replace them. The greatest indignity is that the angels have been subjected to Man's service by guarding him in Paradise. It is these guards that he now dreads as he looks under every bush to find the sleeping serpent so that he can hide in his "mazy folds." He feels completely humiliated that he, who once sat with the highest God, is now incarnated in the shape of a beast. He admits that he is paying the price for his past ambition to aspire to the height of deity. Revenge, though sweet at first, will eventually become bitter. Since God made Man out of the dust to spite Satan and his angels, however, he must repay spite with spite. He finds the serpent sleeping on the "grassy herb" and enters at his mouth.

In the morning Adam and Eve join the "choir of creatures" without human voice and add their "vocal worship" in praise to the Creator. Their discussion then leads them to their work for the day. Eve suggests to Adam that they "divide their labors" since they could get more work accomplished if they were not distracted with each other's conversation and smiles. Though her proposal is admirable in a woman, Adam says, God has not imposed labor so strictly that he would not allow them to talk or smile to refresh each other. Smiles flow from reason and are, therefore, denied to animals. Until they have children who would be able to help them, they can easily keep their paths and bowers from becoming over-grown. He acknowledges, however, that she might be satiated with too much conversation so he could allow her a "short absence" which sometimes makes the return even sweeter. He is troubled that harm will come to her though, since they have already been warned by Raphael about the "malicious foe" that lurks in Para-dise. He urges Eve not to leave his side. Eve tells him she overheard the angel's warning about their enemy and has heard Adam say the same, but she cannot believe that her husband would expect her "firm faith and love" to be shaken by Satan's fraudulent seductions.

To soothe Eve's hurt feelings, Adam answers her with comfort-ing words. It is Satan's attempt that Adam wants to avoid since even that can dishonor her. Adam is confident that the enemy would not dare to assault both of them at once. If he dared, he would surely assault Adam first. The enemy must be subtle if he could seduce angels.

Our foe will not dishonor us, Eve says, but will only turn his foulness on himself. Faith, love, and virtue are of no value if they have not been tested and found to be strong enough to stand on their own worth. God has not given them happiness so frail that either one of them could not stand alone. Adam replies that Man's danger lies within himself, and he can "receive no harm" against his own free will. He warns Eve to use Reason to govern her will but to be sure it does not appear fair when it is false and "misin-forms the will," causing her to disobey God. They should remind each other often, he says, that Reason may "fall into deception." He tells her that if she wants to confirm her constancy, she should prove her obedience. Though she has been forewarned, he will not keep her against her will.

Eve decides to go, confident that a proud foe would not attack the weaker person. Softly she withdraws her hand from Adam's and leaves like a wood nymph (Oread or Dryad) to her groves. Though she looks like the goddess of the hunt (Diana), she is not armed with her bow and quiver for protection but with crude gardening tools instead. Adam bids Eve goodbye with longing looks, remind-ing her to return to him quickly.

Eve has been much deceived, the poet says. She will never again find the tranquility of Paradise, for ambush, in the form of a serpent, lies hidden among the flowers. Since the break of dawn, Satan has been looking for the earthly pair. He hopes to find Eve working separately and, to his surprise, she is alone. She is gently propping up the roses as the serpent draws near. The garden is more lovely than the classical gardens of Adonis and Alcinous, or the biblical garden of Solomon (the sapient king). The serpent admires the garden but is even more attracted to Eve's "heavenly form." Her beauty and "graceful innocence" overpowers his malice, and, for a time, he remains stupefied into good and disarmed of hatred and revenge. The feeling soon ends, however, and "fierce hate" returns.

Since his only pleasure is in destroying, Satan vows he will not pass up the opportunity to perpetrate Eve's ruin and the subsequent death and destruction of all mankind. Though he would shun the intelligence and strength of Adam, Eve is more approachable. He will beguile her with a show of false love since she cannot be "approached by stronger hate." Satan, within the Serpent, is attempting to attract Eve's attention as he "curls his wanton wreath in sight of Eve," but she is too busy to pay attention to the commonplace sounds of the beasts. She finally notices the Serpent when he fawns on her and licks "the ground whereon she trod." Happy that he has gained her attention, the Serpent speaks with flattery, telling her that all living things are gazing at her "celestial beauty." She should be "universally admired," the Serpent says, but here, in this enclosure, she is seen by only one man when she should be adored as a goddess and served by angels.

Eve is surprised to hear a serpent speak since the gift of speech was reserved only for humans on the day of God's creation. She asks him to explain this miracle. Addressing Eve as the "Empress of this fair World," the Tempter tells her that he was just like all the other beasts until one day he came upon a tree whose "alluring fruit" filled him with a "sharp desire." The other beasts could not reach it, but he wound himself around the trunk, plucked the fruit, and ate his fill. He soon felt a "strange alteration" in his ability to reason and became capable of human speech though he retained the shape of a serpent. Flattering Eve, he tells her that of all things "fair and good" in Heaven and Earth, he has found nothing that is equivalent or even comes second to her beauty.

Unwary of the Serpent's deception, Eve asks him to guide her to the tree though she feels his praise is excessive. With a sense of fraudulent hope and joy, the Serpent leads Eve to the Tree of Knowledge. When they arrive, Eve tells him he has wasted his time since God commanded that this is the "tree we may not taste nor touch." The Serpent acts surprised that God should have declared Adam and Eve lords of all the Earth yet forbidden them to eat the fruit. Eve repeats God's command, but the Tempter argues with bold persuasion, telling Eve not to believe God's threats of death. The Serpent has "touched and tasted," yet he has not died. If God were just, he would not hurt them. He has put this prohibition on Adam and Eve because he is afraid they will become "as Gods." If the Serpent, who was a beast, can rise to the level of "brute human," they can be raised to "human Gods," he says. In this way they will die to their humanity and live as Gods. It is God's envy that keeps them in subjection to him, the Serpent says.

The Serpent's words that seem reasonable and truthful win an "easy entrance" into Eve's heart. She gazes longingly at the tempting fruit as noon draws near and stimulates her "eager appetite." The Serpent has shown that eating the fruit did not cause him to die but made him wise instead. She rationalizes her natural desires, seeing the fruit as a cure-all. With "her rash hand" she picks the fruit and eats. Nature then sighed, the poet says, and "gave signs of woe,/ That all was lost."

The guilty Serpent slips back into the thicket, but Eve, with Godhead in her thoughts, does not notice as she gorges herself with the fruit. She worships the tree like a god and promises to sing praises to it each morning. Heaven is "high and remote," and she reasons that God might have been too distant or, perhaps, too busy to notice her evil deed. She deliberates about what she should tell Adam. She considers keeping her new knowledge in her own power and, thereby, render the female sex "more equal," but wonders whether God, having seen, might punish her with death and present Adam with a new Eve. She resolves to share the fruit and her new knowledge with Adam which will cause him to die with her.

Meanwhile, Adam waits anxiously for her return with a garland of flowers for her hair. He has misgivings, however, and goes out to meet her, finding her coming from the Tree of Knowledge with a bough of fruit in her hand. Approaching Adam apologetically, she tells him she has missed him and will never again leave his side. Something strange and wonderful has happened in his absence, however. Contrary to what they have been told, she says, the Serpent has eaten from the forbidden tree and has not died but has taken on human speech and reason instead. He has persuaded her to eat, and she feels the "divine effect" which is close to Godhead. Her cheeks are flushed with guilt and falsehood as she tells Adam she has done it chiefly for him. She offers him the fruit to eat so that they will be equal in degree.

Horror runs through Adam's veins when he hears Eve's story. Dumbfounded, he lets Eve's garland wreath drop from his hands as the faded roses shed from the effects of Eve's fall. Realizing the seriousness of her sinful act, he curses the enemy who has tricked her. He decides immediately that he must die with her since he could not bear to live without her again in the forlorn woods. Even if God gave him another Eve, he could never overcome the loss. Eve is part of his flesh and bone, and he will not part with her.

Resigned to the inevitable, Adam begins to flatter Eve, just as the Serpent had, for being adventurous and bold. What is done cannot be undone, Adam says, and he rationalizes her sin by telling her the Serpent was, after all, the first to profane the fruit by tasting it. Perhaps she will not die since the Serpent still lives. God, in his infinite power, could create more worlds, but he would not allow Satan to triumph over him by crediting him with a second fall.

Overjoyed with Adam's decision, Eve tells him from her own experience that he will not die, but his life will be augmented with new hope. Weeping for joy, she embraces him as she offers him the "enticing fruit." With no scruples he eats against his "better knowledge" as he is "overcome with female charm." Nature gave a second groan, the poet says, as thunder shook the Earth, and the sky wept over Adam's mortal sin.

Acting as if they are intoxicated, Adam and Eve feel lust for each other for the first time. He leads her to a shady bank and "there they fill of love and love's disport/ Took largely." When they become weary with "amorous play," they fall asleep. When they awake from their restless sleep, they realize their loss of innocence and are overcome with guilt, shame, and awareness of their nakedness. Adam is like Samson who, betrayed by Delilah, has been "shorn of his strength." Adam blames Eve for listening to the "false worm" who promised them knowledge of good and evil. They have lost their good and are now evil, he says, which leaves them void of honor and purity. Their loss of innocence has left them aware of their nakedness that they desperately attempt to cover with large leaves from a variety of the fig tree.

Though they have partly covered their shame, their minds are not at ease. For the first time their passion is in subjection to their reason as anger and mistrust comes between them. Adam blames Eve for not listening to him when she wanted them to work separately. Eve, in turn, blames Adam, the head, for not commanding her to stay if he knew the danger was so great. If Adam had been there, she says, he could not have discerned fraud in the Serpent any more than she could.

Incensed, Adam asks her whether this is the thanks he gets for choosing death rather than life after her fall. He had warned her of the danger of the lurking enemy, he says, and if he had forced her he would have been going against her free will. He has made the mistake of thinking she was perfect, but he sees his error now. This is the way it is when a man lets a woman rule, he says. If she goes her own way and then encounters evil, she will blame him for being weak and indulgent. They go on like this, arguing and accusing each other but neither person wins.

Analysis

At the beginning of Book IX (6–12), Milton repeats the theme that was announced in Book I.

> Of Man's first disobedience, and the fruit
> Of that forbidden tree, whose mortal taste
> Brought death into the world, and all our woe,
> With loss of Eden.

P. L., I, 1–4

The theme bears repeating since Book IX is central to the narrative, containing the climax of the action, "Man's first disobedience." The events preceding the climax are a part of the rising action, gradually heightening our emotional response to Eve's temptation and fall and the subsequent fall of Adam. All that follows is a direct consequence of this central climactic event. Milton has been preparing us for this event through the conversation between Adam and Raphael in Books V-VIII. He announces the turning point of the action in Book IX when he explicitly states that "I now must change/ Those notes to tragic." Milton's account of the fall contains the elements of tragedy put forth by Aristotle in the *Poetics*. The fall involves two noble human beings, Adam and Eve, who make a tragic choice that is dictated by some flaw in their character. In this case, both of them subject their reason to their passion. We see evidence of this in Eve's gluttony when she eats the fruit and her vulnerability to the Serpent's flattery as he gains "too easy entrance" into her heart. Adam also lets his passion sway his judgment when he, in his inordinate passion for Eve, quickly resolves to die with her after her fall rather than go on living without her.

These choices result in a tragic catastrophe which is Adam and Eve's loss of immortality and their subsequent expulsion from Paradise. The purpose of classical tragedy is to arouse pity and fear in the reader (or the spectator in drama); sympathize for Eve when she, with a naive trust in the Serpent, reaches for the fruit. The Serpent's lies and flattery lead Eve to believe that he is unselfishly sharing his new-found joy with her, and the dramatic irony reaches its peak when she reasons that he is "far from deceit or guile."

Adam is pitied when he first sees Eve in her lost state. The garland wreath he had prepared for Eve drops from his hands, and the faded roses shed from the effect that Eve's fall has had on him. He cries out in anguish for his loss. "How art thou lost, how on a sudden lost,/ Defaced, deflowered, and now death devot!" The heavy alliteration lends pathos to the language that, of itself, carries overtones of the fading images of death. We pity him for his loss of Eve, but we are aware that it is not only Eve's ruin he must face but his own as well. "And me with thee hath ruined, for with thee/ Certain my resolution is to die." When he faces the choice between what is reasonably right in the sight of God and his

passionate idolatry of Eve, the "fairest of creation," Adam chooses
to die with Eve.

In classical tragedy the reader's emotional conflicts (sins) are
resolved by vicariously expending fear and pity on the tragic heroes. In *Paradise Lost* the reader feels purged of his sins of passion
(pride, gluttony, greed, lust, idolatry) by experiencing them with
Adam and Eve and empathizing with the characters.

It is commonly accepted that Milton had begun composing a
dramatic version of *Paradise Lost* by 1642. The composition of the
epic was begun around 1658 and published in 1667. Milton himself refers to his procrastination in writing his epic through his
"subject for heroic song/ Pleased me long choosing." Though he
had written poetry in his early years, most of the writings of his
middle years dealt with the political and religious issues of his time.
It was not until he was totally blind and retired from political life
that he wrote *Paradise Lost.*

Before entering into the action in Book IX, the poet invokes
his muse for the fourth time (Books I, III, VII, IX). He has called
forth his muse by such various titles as Heavenly muse, Holy Light,
Urania, and now Celestial Patroness. His reference to "her nightly
visitation" is reminiscent of the "Nightly" visits of the Muse in Book
III (32) where he visits the brooks of Sion or, in other words, reads
the Scriptures nightly. In Book IX, however, his muse inspires him
while he is "slumbering." His verse is "unpremeditated" which
implies that he gives little forethought to his writing but depends
largely on spontaneous inspiration.

Images of light and darkness lend contrast to good and evil in
the opening of Book IX. In keeping with the poet's tragic theme in
the introduction, the action opens at midnight with information
regarding Satan's whereabouts. He has spent the last seven days in
darkness within the shadow of the Earth. This alludes to John 4:19.
"Men loved darkness rather than light, because their deeds were
evil." Satan finds an "unsuspected way" into Paradise as he enters
through the underground Tigris River "by stealth." After his soliloquy he searches for the "wily snake" so that he can disguise himself
in its body. "Through each thicket dank or dry,/ Like a black mist
low creeping, he held on/ His midnight search." The language of
the simile reflects the images of darkness and evil: "dank . . . black

mist . . . low creeping," and "midnight" suggest a villainous search. Satan finds the snake and enters its body as he waits for the approach of dawn.

By contrast, dawn in Paradise, before the fall, breaks with "sacred light" that shines on the scented flowers. In the morning all of God's creatures come alive with song. This is reminiscent of the "Holy Light" that emanates from God in the opening lines of Book III (1–3). Milton alludes to the Scriptures where light connotes good and darkness evil. "God is light, and in him is no darkness at all" (I John 1:5).

In Satan's soliloquy he is tormented by the same "bursting passion" that plagued him in Book IV, although now he feels less penitent. He had admitted that "pride and worse ambition threw me down" (P. L., IV, 40). In desperation he had cried out "Is there no place/ Left for repentance?" (79–80). He had considered repentance but finally realized evil must be his good. He now makes a similar statement. "In destroying I find ease." In Book IV he had retained at least a semblance of remorse, but now his attitude has deteriorated to complete hopelessness and despair. Though Earth is appealing at first, he has no desire to dwell on Earth nor in Heaven "unless by mastering Heaven's Supreme" which reminds us of his earlier words, "Better to reign in Hell than serve in Heaven" (P. L., I, 264). His only hope is the glory he will receive among his "infernal Powers" in Hell for ruining mankind. Since his fall he has slowly been degenerating and now he has finally taken the form of a serpent. In his soliloquy he expresses his repulsion in his own words.

> O foul descent! that I who erst contended
> With Gods to sit the highest, am now constrained
> Into a beast, and, mixed with bestial slime.

Incarnating himself as a serpent is the lowest step he has reached in his progressive decline.

When Eve leaves against Adam's advice, to work alone for the day, the poet compares her to Oread, a mountain nymph, or Dryad, a wood nymph, from Greek mythology. She is also seen as Delia, or Diana, Roman goddess of the hunt. Though Eve carries herself with Diana's "goddess-like deport," she is armed only with "garden tools" rather than the "bow and quiver" of Diana. The analogy is clear. Eve, in her naive simplicity, will not be prepared to meet her foe, the subtle serpent, with only a pair of garden tools. The classical reference to Pales, Pomona, and Ceres, goddesses of flocks, fruits, and agriculture respectively, enriches the setting of the pastoral scene.

The garden spot where Eve decides to work is described as a spot "more delicious than those gardens feigned/ Or of revived Adonis." Milton alludes to the beautiful gardens of Adonis and Alcinous and, at the same time, offers a disclaimer of their beauty or worth by telling us they are "feigned." "Revived Adonis" was the youth who, having suffered a mortal wound, was allowed to come to Earth to visit Aphrodite for six months every year. Milton places "the sapient king," King Solomon from the Scriptures, in juxtaposition to the classical allusions to show that Solomon is "not mystic" (mythical) and, therefore, not feigned. In this way he raises the biblical allusions above the level of the heathen, classical ones as he does throughout the epic.

Though Milton follows scriptural authority in the temptation scene (Genesis 3:1–7), he has taken some liberties. It is written in Genesis that "the serpent was more subtil than any beast of the field." Milton elaborates on this passage. Speaking to the Serpent, Eve says, "Thee Serpent, subtlest beast of all the field/ I knew, but not with human voice endued." The Serpent then claims that he is endowed with speech because he has already tasted the fruit of the Tree of Knowledge and, contrary to what God has told them, he has not died. This is a convincing argument for Eve though it deviates from the biblical source. In Genesis Eve takes the Serpent's ability to speak for granted, and the Serpent does not claim to have eaten the fruit, yet Milton uses these points as the Serpent's logical argument to persuade Eve of its divine power in attaining Godhead. If he can become "brute human," the Serpent argues, Eve can become "human God." Concerning the Tree of Knowledge, Eve tells the Serpent, "Ye shall not eat/ Thereof, nor shall ye touch it, lest ye die" which repeats the biblical account almost verbatim. Both accounts also record the Serpent's words to Eve, telling her that God is afraid that if she eats the fruit "ye shall be as Gods." To Milton's claim that Eve's "eager appetite" is stimulated because it is the "hour of noon," there is no parallel in the Scriptures though Genesis refers to the fruit as being "pleasant to the eyes." On the whole, the biblical account is much less dramatic and is written with more economy of language, but Milton generally follows the connotations of the Scriptures, as seen from his seventeenth-century vantage point, throughout the epic.

There is a stark contrast between Adam and Eve before the fall and the unhappy, quarreling pair after they have sinned. Their first reaction to the divine fruit leaves them with an intoxicated feeling. Their passion overcomes their reason and develops into "carnal desire inflaming." He casts "lascivious eyes" on her and "she him/ As wantonly repaid." They burn with lust for each other, but when they awake after their "amorous play," they experience shame and guilt for the first time. Each one blames the other for their blind disobedience to God as they continue their arguing but find no solutions.

Study Questions

1. Why is Book IX a central part of the epic poem?

2. What constitutes the climax of *Paradise Lost*?

3. In what way is Book IX the turning point of the epic?

4. What is Adam and Eve's tragic catastrophe?

5. How does the reader feel purged of his/her own emotional conflicts through the narrative?

6. Where has Satan been hiding for the last seven days?

7. How does Satan enter Paradise?

8. Why is Eve alone on the day of her temptation and fall?

9. According to the Serpent, what will be the effects of eating the fruit from the Tree of Knowledge?

10. What are the effects of the fall on Adam and Eve?

Answers

1. Book IX is central to the poem because it contains the climax of the action.

2. The climax of *Paradise Lost* is "Man's first disobedience" or the fall of Adam and Eve.

3. In Book IX the tone is changed to tragic. All subsequent actions will be affected by the tragic fall in Book IX.

4. Adam and Eve have lost their immortality and will be removed from Paradise.

5. The reader feels purged of his/her own emotional conflicts (sins) by empathizing with the tragic hero.

6. Satan has been traveling within the dark shadow of the Earth.

7. Satan enters Paradise through the underground fountain of the Tigris River.

8. Eve has suggested to Adam that they work separately so they can get more work done.

9. The Serpent tells Eve the fruit from the Tree of Knowledge will make her like a god.

10. Adam and Eve begin quarreling and blaming each other for their lost state.

Suggested Essay Topics

1. The poet is changing his "notes to tragic" in Book IX. Explain how the fall of Adam and Eve is a classical tragedy. What tragic choices do each of them make and how does it affect the catastrophe? How does the reader feel purged after he/she has read the epic poem? Cite examples from the poem to explain your answer.

2. Images of light and darkness represent contrasts of good and evil in Book IX. Describe Satan in his world of evil. How are the images of darkness symbolic of Satan's travels for the past seven days? Explain the images of darkness. Explain the images of light in Paradise. Support your answer with examples from the poem.

Book X

Summary

Since nothing escapes the eye of the omniscient God, it is known in Heaven that the Serpent has perverted Eve and she has, in turn, tempted Adam to taste the "fatal fruit." God has not hindered Satan from tempting Adam and Eve, however. In his wisdom and justice, God has armed them with free will, but they have chosen to disobey him and have, therefore, deserved to fall.

The guardian angels from Paradise arrive in Heaven with the sad news. They are greeted by multitudes of angels who are displeased but also show pity for Adam and Eve. God's voice appears from a cloud amidst the thunder, and the angels gather to listen. God calms the angels' fears and tells the guards of Paradise that what has taken place could not have been prevented. He has known all along that Satan would prevail in his attempt to seduce Man and cause him to fall. Man was governed by his own free will, however, and sentence must now be passed on his transgression. Though death has already been determined, it has not yet been inflicted. God appoints the Son as Mediator to administer justice as well as mercy to Adam and Eve. The Son is considered to be Man's friend since he has already volunteered to give himself as a ransom for Man's sin.

The Son arrives on Earth in the cool of the evening. When Adam and Eve hear him walking in the garden, they hide in the thickest part of the forest. The Son calls Adam's name with a loud voice, and they both appear with guilty looks. Adam tells the Son he was afraid of him and hid himself because he was naked. The Son asks whether he has eaten the forbidden fruit and, therefore, realizes he is naked. Adam deliberates, wondering whether to take all the blame himself and protect Eve by concealing her guilt or whether to tell the truth. He finally decides to tell the Son that Eve offered him the fruit and he ate, but the Son rebukes him, asking him whether Eve is his God whom he must obey. He tells Adam he should love Eve but not be held in subjection to her. She was not meant to rule, the Son says, since that is Adam's part by nature.

The Son then asks Eve what she has done, and she replies that the Serpent beguiled her. Promptly passing judgment on the Serpent, the Son dooms him to grovel on his belly and eat dust for the rest of his days. The Son also proclaims that hatred will exist between Eve's descendants and the Serpent's offspring. Turning to Eve, he decrees the pain of childbirth and the submission to her husband's will as punishment for her sin. He declares that Adam shall earn his bread by the sweat of his brow until he returns to the ground that God used for his creation.

After Adam and Eve have been judged, the Son tells them that their deaths will be far in the future. Feeling pity for them, he dresses them with the "skins of beasts" that have either been killed or have shed their skins. He also clothes their "inward nakedness" with his "robe of righteousness" before he ascends into Heaven.

Meanwhile, Sin becomes restless as a mysterious force is drawing her to "things of like kind." She reveals her plan to her son, Death, to build a highway from the gates of Hell to Earth where Satan, their father, now resides. Death agrees to do his equal share as he sniffs the air for the smell of mortal carcasses that he will feed on when he arrives on Earth. "Following the track/ Of Satan," Sin and Death build a broad high-arched bridge across the Abyss. Along the way they meet Satan who is escaping the judgment of the Son of God in Eden. Though he is disguised as a bright angel, they recognize him immediately and greet him with joy. Sin attributes the highway to Satan's success on Earth and salutes him as the monarch of Hell and all the World. Satan gives Sin and Death his blessing and sends them off to Paradise to "reign in bliss" as he continues his journey on the highway to Hell.

Disguised as a common military angel, Satan arrives in Pandemonium and mounts his throne. He reveals himself as his head slowly appears out of a cloud, and he is greeted with cheers and congratulations. Addressing the fallen angels, he promises to lead them out of Hell to their newly acquired world. He lies as he tells them how much pain and suffering he has endured on his crude passage through the Abyss, but now, he says, the way has been paved to expedite their "glorious march" out of Hell. Satan tells them of his fraudulent seductions of Man which separated him from his creator. What is even more strange, and perhaps laughable, is that Man and all of God's world has now been given to the powers of Hell, and Satan has done it with an apple. God judged

the Serpent but only with a bruise, Satan says, and who would not purchase a world for a mere bruise. Satan expects applause but all he gets is a "dismal universal hiss" because he and his angels are all being transformed into serpents. God is passing judgment on them as he had promised, and he now lures them to a grove of trees resembling the Tree of Knowledge, but as they eagerly eat the fruit, it turns into "bitter ashes."

Meanwhile, Sin and Death arrive in Paradise. Sin asks Death what he thinks of their empire, but he says it matters little where he stays as long as he can satisfy his ravenous appetite. Sin tells him to feed on the vegetation and beasts until she can infect Man, and he will be the "sweetest prey."

God observes the "waste and havoc brought about by the "dogs of Hell," but promises that the Son will eventually be victorious over them and hurl Sin and Death through Chaos, sealing up the gates of Hell forever. The heavenly chorus responds with halleluiahs to the Son. God then orders the angels to regulate the sun and create changeable weather. Some say the angels inclined the axis of the Earth over 20 degrees, and some say they steered the sun off its course and brought about the change of seasons, the poet says.

Discord, the daughter of Sin, causes the animals to fight and devour each other and flee in fear of Man or glare at him as he passes by. These are the "growing miseries" Adam observes from his hiding place in the gloomy shade. He cries out in pain, mourning the loss of his "glorious World" and his communion with God. He sees no reason to propagate the race if it will only bring curses on his head. He tells his Maker he did not ask to become Man. He finally concedes that his punishment is nevertheless just, but he still sees no reason to prolong his life as long as he knows Death is coming. He wishes he could die, but one thought still plagues him—that the spirit of Man might not perish with his physical body, and he will die a "deathless death." He wonders whether God's anger will never be satisfied and why he must punish all mankind for one man's sin.

As he curses the day he was created, Eve approaches with soft words, but he orders her out of his sight. Calling her a serpent, he rails at her "inward fraud" that is disguised in her "heavenly form." He wonders why God, who created all the spirits masculine, placed "this fair defect/ Of Nature," Woman, in Paradise. Eve is in tears and falls at Adam's feet, begging him to forgive her and not forsake her. She loves him sincerely and pleads that they might live in peace for the short time they have left. She admits having sinned against God and Adam and wishes the sentence could fall on her alone. Eve's words soften Adam's anger, and he vows that all the blame should fall on his head rather than hers. He proposes that they put blame aside and lighten each other's burden. Eve then suggests that, with Adam's approval, they either remain childless by abstaining from "nuptial embraces," or take their own lives to keep from bringing a cursed race into the world.

Offering a "safer resolution," Adam cautions Eve that suicide is not an escape from God. If Eve's "seed shall bruise/ The Serpent's head," then they will avenge themselves on the Serpent by propagating the race who will eventually defeat Satan and his evil powers. In the meantime they will learn about fire and how to deal with inclement weather. "What better can we do," Adam says, than to bow humbly before God and ask for his pardon. They both fall prostrate on the ground and humbly confess their sins.

Analysis

Immediately after Eve eats the fruit in Book IX, she reflects briefly on God's ability to see her sinful act. Rationalizing that Heaven is "High and remote" (P. L., IX, 812), she dismisses her fear and turns her thoughts to Adam. In Book X, nothing "can scape the eye/ Of God all-seeing," and her forbidden act is soon known in all of Heaven. Adam and Eve, though tempted by the Serpent, have exercised their own free will when they disobeyed God, and they must now be judged. God sends the Son to Earth to administer "justice with mercy."

Betrayed by his guilt, Adam can no longer hide his nakedness and must confess to the Son what he has done. "She gave me of the tree, and I did eat." The Son counters Adam's excuse with a sharp rebuke: "Was she thy God?" He tells Adam that God set him above Eve as her superior, and it is his duty to rule her rather than be subject to her rule. She should "attract/ Thy love, not thy subjection." This is reminiscent of Adam's discussion with Raphael in Book VIII. The words are almost identical. Eve is "worthy well/ Thy cherishing, thy honoring, and thy love,/ Not thy subjection" (68–70). Adam has made the mistake of exalting Eve above her place in the scale of nature. With their fall, the hierarchy has been broken and tragedy is the result. The scale of Nature has been reviewed in Book V where Milton gives an elaborate description of the various degrees in the hierarchy, impressing upon the reader that the lower forms of Nature must never usurp the power of the higher ones (469–505). This idea harks back to ancient times, the days of Aristotle, and was still being revered in the seventeenth century. It must be understood that in the epic, Milton is setting before the reader an accepted seventeenth-century ideal of male/female relationships. Helen Gardner points out that "Eve sinned by being 'bold and adventurous,' qualities Milton, with his age, thought inappropriate in a woman. Adam sinned by being dependent on another, a quality inappropriate in a man" (Helen Gardner, "The Human Theme," 90). Adam falls because he cannot live without Eve (P. L., IX, 908), and she falls because she dares to "work separately" (P. L., IX, 424).

In his other writings Milton occasionally abandons the commonly held ideas about sex roles that are set forth in *Paradise Lost*. In "Tetrachordon," for example, he discusses the idea of wives being subject to their husbands and denies that this is always the case. "Not but that particular exceptions may have place, if she exceed her husband in prudence and dexterity, and he contentedly yield: for then a superior and more natural law comes in, that the wiser should govern the less wise, whether male or female" ("Tetrachordon," IV). These are exceptions, Milton says, rather than the rule.

When Eve shamefully admits that "the Serpent me beguiled and I did eat," the Son promptly judges the Serpent, in his absence, sentencing him to grovel on his belly for the remainder of his days. There will be hatred and strife between Satan and the Woman, the Son says. "Her seed shall bruise thy head, thou bruise his heel." Milton alludes to Genesis 3:15 in this passage, repeating it almost verbatim. The Serpent (Satan) will be defeated by the future generations of Eve. Jesus will triumph over Satan, "prince of the air," whose kingdom will be usurped as he falls "like lightning down from Heaven." This will be a fulfillment of the prophecy, recorded in Luke 10:18. "And he said unto them, I beheld Satan as lightning fall from heaven."

Satan's evil deed on Earth has not only established him as the Prince of Darkness, widening his vast empire to include Earth and Hell, but has given his offsprings, Sin and Death, the legacy of his "infernal empire," as well. They will rule the "race of Satan" on Earth, and the three will have dominion over Hell and all the world. Rajan appropriately refers to Satan, Sin, and Death as the "infernal trinity" (B. Rajan, *Paradise Lost and the Seventeenth Century Reader*, 77). As the "Antagonist of Heaven's Almighty King," Satan's plan to lead a "glorious march" to Earth on a newly paved highway is foiled as his infernal kingdom degenerates into a race of serpents, turning his triumph into shame. "A greater power" rules them and, just as the Son had decreed, they are destined to crawl on their bellies and eat the dust for the rest of their days. Satan's metamorphosis into a lowly serpent is the last stage of his progressive degeneration that has been taking place since his arrival in Hell in Book I. His form in the body of a serpent now conforms to the evil that is inside of him. Edmund Spenser, a contemporary of Milton, has set this Platonic idea into verse.

> For of the soule the bodie forme doth take:
> For soule is forme, and doth the bodie make
> *An Hymne in Honor of Beautie*, 132–33.

Spenser expresses the idea that spirit and matter are interconnected.

After the fall there was a change of weather on Earth, the poet says, bringing harsh winters and hot summers. It is rumored that the angels slanted the Earth's axis slightly more than 20 degrees or perhaps the sun was set to fluctuate its movements north and south of the equator, causing the change of seasons. Before the fall there were flowers and trees in a world of eternal spring, but now Adam and Eve must contend with the extremes of weather. When the Son comes to Earth to administer justice to Adam and Eve, he pities them because they stand "before him naked to the air, that now/ Must suffer change." He clothes them in skins of beasts to cover their nakedness and ward off the cold.

Discord, the daughter of Sin, resides on Earth after the fall and brings Death among the animals. For the first time, they fight and kill each other and run away from Man out of fear.

In his long soliloquy (124 lines), Adam struggles with the difficult problem of death. He considers death a mockery and would welcome the end of his life that is nothing but the "cruel expectation" of his inevitable death and that of his offspring. He is plagued by one doubt—that his spirit will not die with his body, and he will "die a living death." He vacilates back and forth indecisively until he finally concludes, with little conviction, that "all of me then shall die . . . since human reach no further knows." This is comparable to Hamlet's plaintive cry when he considers suicide as an end to his miserable existence but is held back by his fear that death may not be the end.

> But that the dread of something after death,
> The undiscover'd country, from whose bourn
> No traveller returns, puzzles the will,
> And makes us rather bear those ills we have,
> Than fly to others that we know not of?
> Shakespeare, Hamlet, 77–81

Like Hamlet, Adam is afraid he will die a "deathless death" where God might "extend/ His sentence beyond dust." Out of the depths of despair, Adam finally recognizes his guilt and concedes that his punishment is just, and he is later led to repentence. At the end of Book X he again falls prostrate on the ground before God, but his mood reflects one of repentence rather than despair.

Study Questions

1. Who is sent from Heaven to judge Adam and Eve after the fall?

2. What is Adam and Eve's punishment for their disobedience to God?

3. How does the Son judge the Serpent (Satan) for tempting Eve?

4. What do Sin and Death do to make Earth more accessible?

5. What will Eve's descendants do to the Serpent's offspring?

6. Who helps to bring Adam out of the depths of despair?

7. How does Death feel about his new empire on Earth?

8. What does Discord do on Earth after the fall?

9. What happens to Satan and his fallen angels when he arrives in Hell?

10. What happens to the fruit that is eaten by the serpents in Hell?

Answers

1. God sends the Son to judge Adam and Eve after the fall.

2. Eve will bear the pain of childbirth and the subjection to her husband's will. Adam will labor by the sweat of his brow to earn his bread.

3. The Serpent will crawl on his belly and eat dust for the rest of his days.

4. Sin and Death pave a highway for easier access from Hell to Earth.

5. The descendants of Eve will destroy the Serpent's evil offspring.

6. Eve asks Adam to forgive her and volunteers to take all the blame which brings Adam out of his despair.

7. Death says he would be equally as happy in Hell, Earth, or Heaven as long as he could satisfy his insatiable appetite.

8. Discord causes the animals to fight and kill each other and develop a fear of Man.

9. Satan and his fallen angels are all turned into serpents which was a fulfillment of the Son's judgment.

10. The fruit that the serpents eat turns to ashes.

Suggested Essay Topics

1. The Son pronounces judgment on the Serpent, telling him that the Woman's "seed shall bruise thy head, thou bruise

his heel." Explicate this passage in the light of Eve's descendants. According to the prophecy, what will happen to Satan and his evil powers? What part will Jesus play in the fulfillment of the prophecy? Cite examples from the epic to support your answer.

2. In his soliloquy Adam struggles with his doubts about death. Compare his fears to those of Shakespeare's Hamlet in his famous soliloquy beginning "To be or not to be." What do both Adam and Hamlet have in common concerning death? Is the mystery of death unique only to them? In what way is it a universally human mystery? How does Adam resolve his problem? Use examples from the epic to support your view.

Book XI

Summary

Adam and Eve now stand repentant before God who has sent his prevenient grace down from Heaven to soften their hearts. Their prayers are heard by the Son who intercedes for them, asking for their peaceful reconciliation with God. Though he grants them forgiveness, God will not allow them to remain in Paradise because its "pure immortal elements" will no longer mix with their sinful nature. God has provided Death as Man's "final remedy" which will be followed by a "second life" for the just who live by faith.

God then calls an assembly of his heavenly angels to inform them of his judgment of mankind. To prevent Adam and Eve from tasting the fruit of the Tree of Life and, thereby, living in their sinful state forever, God decrees that they be removed from the garden. He appoints the archangel Michael to "drive out the sinful pair" but to soften the "sad sentence" and console them by revealing to Adam what the future will hold for them and their descendants. God will "enlighten" Michael as he foretells the future of mankind. Michael should again remind Adam and Eve of God's covenant to destroy Satan and his evil powers through Eve's offspring. The east gate of the garden must be closely guarded to keep the foul spirits from entering. Michael prepares to go, taking four Cherubim along to assist him.

Meanwhile, Adam and Eve greet the morning after their night of prayer. With renewed hope, Adam addresses Eve as the "Mother of all Mankind" whose offspring will destroy Satan and his evil powers. With humility Eve replies that she does not deserve such a title. Since she was the one who first brought Death into the world, she should not be honored as the "source of life." Though they have had a sleepless night, the morning again calls them to their labors. Determined never to leave Adam's side again, Eve suggests that they live contentedly in their fallen state, enjoying the "pleasant walks of Paradise." Adam senses a bad omen, however, when the eagle and the lion hunt their prey for the first time.

Adam predicts a "further change" and his fears are not unfounded as a group of angels arrive from Heaven and land on a hill in Paradise. The archangel Michael approaches and Adam goes to meet him, telling Eve to stay behind. He looks more majestic than Raphael, and Adam fears that there will be some new laws imposed on them. Adam bows low as he meets Michael who does not appear in the shape of an angel but is dressed as a kingly young man in military attire.

Michael begins by telling Adam his prayers have been heard, and, though his sentence is death, by God's grace, he will be given enough time to cover his one sinful act with "many deeds well done." He has come to remove Adam and Eve from Paradise since God will not permit them to stay any longer. Surprised and heartbroken, Adam stands speechless, but Eve can be heard in the background, lamenting the loss of Paradise which is a blow "worse than Death." Michael gently tells Eve that she will be going with her husband whom she is obligated to follow. Wherever he goes, she must consider that place as her native soil. Recovering from his shock, Adam humbly thanks Michael for his gentleness in breaking the news of their removal from Eden. He regrets leaving his familiar surroundings, but his biggest loss will be the presence of God. Michael tells him God is omnipresent, and he will be in the valley and the plain just as he has been in Paradise.

Michael puts Eve into a deep sleep as he leads Adam to the highest hill in Eden to inform him about future generations. Removing the film from Adam's eyes that has been caused by his sin, Michael replaces it with three drops from the well of life. Adam

falls into a trance, but Michael lifts him, asking him to observe what he will now show him. Adam is first shown the vision of Cain murdering his brother Abel out of jealousy. Adam is terrified at his first sight of death and cannot understand the justice of an evil man, Cain, murdering a good man, Abel. Michael replies that these brothers are his sinful offspring, but the bloody act will someday be avenged. Adam asks whether he has now seen Death, and Michael replies that there are many forms of Death. Immediately a vision of a lazer-house filled with people afflicted with various diseases appears before Adam's eyes, showing him what misery the inabstinence of Eve can cause. Adam weeps out of compassion for their sufferings and wonders why Man, created in God's image, should be forced to endure such degradation. Michael replies that it was not God's likeness but their own they disfigured by their "ungoverned appetite," a vice attributed "mainly to the sin of Eve." They have perverted God's image in themselves by refusing to follow "Nature's healthful rules." Adam admits that it is just, but wonders if there is no other way to die. Michael replies that Death takes many shapes, and if he lives a temperate life, he will reach old age, although he then must endure the loss of his youth and slowly lose touch with his senses. Michael tells him not to love nor hate his life, but live it well for as long as he is given life.

Michael then shows him another vision of a plain, dotted with tents of various colors. Melodious harp and organ music is playing. A group of devoutly religious men appear, and out of the tents licentious women, adorned with jewels and "wanton dress," sing and dance for them. Each man chooses a woman who lures him into her tent. Adam is delighted at this sight since it is much more peaceful than the last two visions of hatred and death. Michael admonishes him for looking only for the pleasure in life. Those were "tents/ Of wickedness," he says, where the seeming goddesses were actually lustful women, causing the "Sons of God" to yield their virtue to them. Adam then understands that a Man's woe always begins with a Woman, but Raphael corrects him. Man's woe begins with his own "effeminate slackness," he says.

Adam is shown another scene where a race of giants is at war, and slaughter and carnage are everywhere. A council is held to settle the dispute when one middle-aged man rises to negotiate peace and speak the truth. He is taken away to Heaven in a cloud, however, and the violence continues. In tears, Adam laments their inhumane treatment; Michael tells him these are the children of those ill-mated marriages he saw in the tents. The righteous man he saw in the vision was hated for being the only one to tell the truth.

The vision of war disappears and Adam is shown the life of people who wile away their time in luxurious, sinful pleasures. Noah calls them to conversion and repentance, but they refuse to listen. He is the only righteous man left in a world of evil. He builds an ark and when all his goods, animals, and family are aboard, God seals the door. When the flood comes, all people are drowned except Noah and his family.

When Adam sees the end of all his offspring, he weeps again and wishes he had not seen the visions of the future. It is enough to bear things one day at a time, Adam says, but he asks Michael to unfold the rest of the story just the same. The storm is abated and the retreating sea leaves the ark on a mountain top. A messenger, in the form of a dove, is sent out and returns with an olive branch. Dry ground appears, and Noah and his family disembark. Adam rejoices that God would now "raise another world" from one just man. He questions the meaning of the rainbow and Michael explains that it is God's covenant that he will never again destroy the Earth by flood. It is not until the last days that fire will purge both Heaven and Earth where the just shall dwell forever.

Analysis

In the first edition of *Paradise Lost*, the last two books were included in Book X. Milton divided this book into three sections for his second edition to include Books XI and XII not only because Book X had been relatively lengthy, but also for structural reasons. In Book XI Michael presents the biblical history to Adam in visions, and in Book XII he simply narrates the biblical events. Only five lines were added to the second edition in which Milton notes the shift from the "world destroyed" after the fall to the "world restored" (P. L., XII, 3) after Christ's resurrection.

Many commentators have criticized the last two books of *Paradise Lost*, seeing them as an accessory to the epic since the fall has already taken place along with Adam and Eve's judgment and con-

sequent repentance. For an understanding of Book XI, it is necessary to return to Milton's theme in Book I. "Of Man's first
disobedience, and the fruit/ Of that forbidden tree, whose mortal
taste/ Brought death into the world, and all our woe" (P. L., I, 1–3).
Adam's visions of future generations in Book XI are a living example
of the "death" and "woe" that has been brought about by his disobedience and fall. By vicariously experiencing the sorrows in these
visions of human history—murder, disease, prostitution, idle pleasures, and war—Adam sees the magnitude of his sin and slowly
gains a clearer understanding of the justification for his expulsion
from Paradise. God has commanded Michael to drive Adam and
Eve out of Paradise "though sorrowing, yet in peace." It is Michael's
duty to help them see their loss of Paradise as a just punishment,
but he must not destroy their hope for God's plan of redemption
that is set forth in Book XII. Milton's purpose in his epic is to "justify the ways of God to men" (P. L., I, 26). Michael must, therefore,
help Adam understand that God administers mercy along with
justice. Adam cannot fully comprehend the prophecy of God's re-
demptive mercy through his Son in Book XII until he experiences
shame and despair for the wide-scale misery he has caused by his
sin of disobedience.

At the beginning of Book XI, the tone changes from the hopelessness and despair seen in Adam's soliloquy in the previous book,
to that of repentance and hope. Adam addresses Eve as the "Mother
of all Mankind." It is through Eve's offspring that Man will live again.
God has promised that "thy seed shall bruise our foe," Adam says,
and Eve is humbled by the fact that she, who brought death on all
mankind, should now be honored as "the source of Life." When
Adam prefaces his greeting to Eve with "hail to thee,/ Eve," we are
reminded of Raphael's comparable greeting to Eve in Book V.

> On whom the Angel "Hail"
> Bestowed, the holy salutation used
> Long after to blest Mary, second Eve.
>   P. L., V, 385–87

In Book XI we again identify Eve with Mary, the second Eve, whose
seed (Christ) will crush Satan's strength by defeating Sin and Death.

It is ironic that Eve is associated with Sin, Death, and the fall, but, at the same time, holds the promise of redemption and life as the "Mother of all things living."

Adam approaches the archangel Michael with some reservation, seeing him as a majestic-looking monarch who brings "great tidings" from God's throne. He does not appear as the "sociably mild" Raphael with whom he has shared food and pleasant conversation in Books V-VIII. The seriousness of Michael's mission, Adam and Eve's expulsion from Paradise, lends an air of solemnity and awe to his manly appearance. Unlike Raphael, God's spirit will be with him to inspire him in his somber task. "I shall thee enlighten." This forewarns us that Michael's task is of a divine nature. When he arrives, Michael needs "no preface" but goes straight to the business at hand. He minces no words, promptly informing Adam and Eve that, although grace has been granted, they must leave Paradise. In administering God's punishment, it is logical that Michael would be portrayed with more severity than Raphael.

Though he has heard much about Death as the punishment for his sin, Adam finally sees Death for the first time when Michael presents the scene of the evil brother murdering the one who is righteous. This alludes to the story of the first murder in Genesis. "Cain rose up against Abel his brother, and slew him" (Genesis 4:8). Adam is appalled at the injustice of the evil man killing the upright one who was devoted to God. Michael informs Adam that these brothers will be his offspring. He points out that, though the bloody deed will be avenged at the time of judgment, justice is not necessarily carried out in a sinful world.

As Michael presents the vision of war, Adam experiences another heartrending reflection of a chaotic world with death and destruction at every hand. In the midst of the carnage, however, one man speaks out for justice, truth, and peace but is snatched up in a cloud and taken to Heaven. This is an allusion to Enoch who was a righteous man. "And Enoch walked with God: and he was not; for God took him" (Genesis 5:24). Noah too is the "one just man alive" who stands alone as an example of righteousness in a dark age of licentiousness and moral degradation. He preaches conversion and repentance but, like Enoch, no one will listen to him. Milton is fond of the moral image of one righteous man who

stands alone against the hostile crowd. Abdiel's independent rebuke of Satan's heresy against God in the war in Heaven has been
reviewed elsewhere in the text. Abdiel was also the only dissenter.
"Among the faithless, faithful only he" (P. L., V, 896). The final ex-
emplar, an even greater man (Christ), will be revealed in Book XII.

Study Questions

1. Who is sent to Earth to tell Adam and Eve about their expulsion from Paradise?

2. In what form does Michael appear on Earth?

3. What is Adam's reaction when he is told that he must leave
   Paradise?

4. According to Michael, where can God be found?

5. Where is Eve while Adam and Michael discuss future events?

6. What method does Michael use to reveal the future to Adam?

7. Who are the two just men from the Bible who stand alone in
   Book XI?

8. What is Adam's first real example of Death in the vision?

9. What is a lazer-house?

10. Why does God send the rainbow to Noah after the flood?

Answers

1. The archangel Michael is sent to Earth to break the sad news
   of Adam and Eve's expulsion from Paradise.

2. Michael appears on Earth in the form of a man dressed in
   military attire.

3. Adam reacts with shocked silence at first but soon tells
   Michael that his greatest regret is leaving God.

4. Michael tells Adam that God is omnipresent and will be on
   the plain as well as in Paradise.

5. Michael has put Eve into a deep sleep.

6. Michael presents visions of biblical history to Adam to reveal the future of the World.

7. Two biblical examples of men who stand alone against the crowd are Noah and Enoch.

8. Adam's first real example of death is Cain, an evil man, murdering his brother Abel, a just man.

9. A lazer-house is an institution filled with people afflicted with various diseases.

10. God sends the rainbow as a covenant that he will never again destroy the people of the Earth by flood.

Suggested Essay Topics

1. It has been suggested that Books XI and XII are unnecessary to the structure of *Paradise Lost*. Explain the function of Book XI. How can it be seen as an integral part of the theme? In what way does it contribute to the characterization of Adam? How does it help us to understand Adam's development? How does it prepare Adam for his expulsion from Paradise? Cite examples from the poem to explain your answer.

2. Milton is fond of the idea of "one just man" who stands for his beliefs against a hostile world. Discuss this idea in the light of Noah and Enoch. Are their stories applicable to today's world? How can their experiences be applied to modern society? Do we still see people who stand alone in the face of opposition? Give examples from the poem to support your view.

Book XII

Summary

After the vision of Noah and the destruction of the world by flood, Michael pauses for a moment to give Adam an opportunity to ask further questions. Since he does not respond, Michael hurries on to resume the story of human history, but instead of showing the events he will now tell about them.

With the judgment of God by flood still fresh in their minds, Noah's descendants live righteous and peaceful lives, Michael says, until Nimrod, ambitious for power, rises up in rebellion to God. To make a name for himself that will be remembered throughout the world, he gathers a crew to help him build the Tower of Babel "whose top may reach to Heaven." It is made from brick and the bituminous elements that boil onto the plain from the mouth of Hell. Before the tower is completed, however, God intervenes, confusing their native language so that the builders cannot communicate. Feeling mocked by God, they angrily leave the ridiculous tower unfinished.

Displeased with his descendant, Adam criticizes Nimrod for usurping the authority of God who has given Man dominion over beast, fish, and fowl but has not made him lord over other men. Adam is appalled at the insolence of a wretched man who would think that he could encroach upon Heaven and defy God. He argues that the air is too thin above the clouds, and there is no food to sustain men at that height. Michael replies that Adam's accusation of Nimrod is justified, but he must remember that "rational liberty" along with "right reason" was lost after the fall, and men and government are often controlled by their passions. Sometimes nations become tyrannical as is the case with the "irreverent son" of Noah, Ham, whose people and their succeeding generations are cursed to become a race of servants.

The world goes "from bad to worse" until God, weary of people's immorality, resolves to leave them to their own wicked ways and focus his attention on "a mighty nation," Israel, that springs from "one faithful man," Abraham. His race is blessed with the seed that will produce the "great Deliverer, who shall bruise/ The Serpent's head," Michael says, but this will be revealed to Adam more clearly at another time.

Moses is later sent by God to deliver his people out of captivity in Egypt and into the promised land. Extending his rod over the Red Sea, Moses, with God's power, parts the sea and the Israelites march safely through on dry land to Canaan on the other side. The Egyptians, led by Pharaoh, follow in pursuit but are swallowed up by the sea as Moses bids the waters return. The Israelites found their government in the wilderness, and Moses establishes the Ten Commandments, ordained by God on Mount Sinai, as their laws. A tabernacle is built to house the ark containing the testimony of God's covenant "promised to Abraham and his seed."

Adam replies that he now sees how all the nations will be blessed through Abraham, but he still does not understand why so many laws are needed. Many laws indicate sins, and he wonders how God can tolerate such sinful people. Michael tells Adam that the laws govern them only until they can move "from inposition of strict laws, to free/ Acceptance of large grace." It is, therefore, not Moses who leads his people into Canaan, Michael says, but Joshua, who comes later. Judges and kings then rule the Israelites, and from the royal stock of King David, the "Woman's Seed" will produce a kingdom without end. David's son Solomon, famous for his wealth and wisdom, builds a "glorious temple" where he places the Ark of the Covenant. The "foul idolatries" of Solomon's subjects "so incense God," however, that he allows them to be taken to Babylon and held in captivity for 70 years. Upon return, they live moderately for a few years, but dissension, starting among the priests, soon grows among them, and they lose the kingdom to foreign powers. "Barred of his right" to inherit the royal kingdom, the Messiah is born of a virgin, and his Sire is the "Power of the Most High."

Adam now understands God's divine promise concerning the future "Seed of Woman" but is still confused about "what stroke shall bruise the Victor's heel." Michael tells him the Serpent is not overcome in a duel with Christ. Satan's head is not literally trampled under Christ's heel, but, metaphorically speaking, Christ bruises the head of Satan by rising from the dead and in this way crushes his strength by defeating Sin and Death. Through his death on the cross, Christ pays the ransom for Adam's sin which brought Death into the world, Michael says. Ironically, he is "slain for bringing life" to mankind.

Christ is raised from the dead and enters Heaven to sit at God's right hand. In the last days he will judge the living and the dead and reward the faithful. At that time this Earth will be a far happier Paradise than the present Eden. Adam responds joyfully, praising God that so much good can come out of evil, but wonders what happens to the faithful followers of Christ left on Earth after His ascension into Heaven. Michael tells him they have been persecuted, but God sends his Spirit to guide them to truth as faith works through love in their hearts and gives them power "to resist/ Satan's assaults." The Holy Spirit is first given to the Apostles and then to all who are baptized. When the Apostles die, corrupt priests take over as teachers and, like sly wolves, pervert the truth of the Scriptures with man-made traditions. Those who persevere, worshipping in Spirit and in Truth, bear "heavy persecution." The world will go on like this until the day that the wicked will be avenged and the just rewarded with eternal life.

Adam feels he has all the knowledge he can absorb and is comforted by the fact that he will now leave Paradise with peace of mind. He has learned that "to obey is best," and he must continue to love the only true God. "Suffering for truth's sake" is the "highest victory" and to those who remain faithful, Death is the gate to eternal life. Michael commends him for attaining "the sum/ Of wisdom." If he adds faith, virtue, patience, temperance, and love to his knowledge, he will not mind leaving Paradise, for he will possess a Paradise within himself.

As they descend from the hill, they find Eve awake and well-rested. God has given her a comforting dream in which she "the Promised seed shall all restore." They are now ready to leave Paradise as the Cherubim stand watch, and God's brandished sword blazes like a comet high in front of them. Michael takes each of them by the hand, leading them through the eastern gate and down the cliff to the plain and then disappears. "Looking back," Adam and Eve shed "some natural tears" as they "through Eden took their solitary way."

Analysis

The dramatic structure of the last two books of *Paradise Lost* is considered the *denouement* or the unraveling of the plot of the narrative. After the climax, the fall of Adam and Eve in Book IX, the final books give Adam a vivid clarification and a necessary perspective of the dire consequences of his fall. Michael has used the device of visions in Book XI to drive home to Adam the far-reaching extent of the misery and suffering in a sinful world. He now shifts to a strictly narrative approach, changing his emphasis from a "world destroyed" to a "world restored." Adam's moral instruction must necessarily include hope for his lost condition to prepare him for his expulsion from Paradise. He comes to a full understanding of that hope when Michael helps him realize that it is Christ's resur-

rection that crushes the Serpent's head by defeating Sin and Death. He sees the significance of his own role in God's master plan of redemption when he finally comprehends the lineage of Christ.

> yet from my loins
> Thou (Virgin Mother) shalt proceed,
> and from thy womb the Son
> Of God Most High; so God with Man unites.

Michael's education of Adam accomplishes God's intent for Adam and Eve; to send them out of Paradise "though sorrowing, yet in peace" (P. L., XI, 117). Adam himself verifies this. "Greatly instructed I shall hence depart,/ Greatly in peace of thought, and have my fill/ Of knowledge."

After the destruction of the world by flood, Michael says, Noah's descendants, still living in fear of God's judgment, lead their lives peacefully and productively. One man, "a mighty hunter," soon rises up in rebellion against God, however, building a tower "whose top may reach to Heaven." This alludes to the Scriptures. "He began to be a mighty one in the earth . . . Even as Nimrod the mighty hunter before the Lord. And the beginning of his kingdom was Babel" (Genesis 10:9–10). Nimrod, who built the Tower of Babel, was also building a powerful empire and held men in "subjection to his empire tyrannous." Many commentators see Milton's contemporary reference to Charles I in the story of Nimrod.

> Or from Heaven claiming second sovranty;
> And from rebellion shall derive his name,
> Though of rebellion others he accuse.

By claiming to receive his divine authority from God, the tyrant (Charles I) not only rebel falsely but also accuses the leaders of the Puritan Revolution of rebellion. Milton is sure to point out that Nimrod was dealt with by God just as he will deal with tyrants of his own time who attempt to destroy Man's liberty. He punctuates this idea through Adam. Remembering God's earlier injunction before the fall, Adam says that God has given authority over beast, fish, and fowl, "but man over men/ He made not lord." This type of tyranny can only be attributed to the fall, Michael says.

After Christ's ascension into Heaven, the Holy Spirit is sent to the Apostles to evangelize the nations. They baptize people and after they have performed Christ's ministry, they die. In their place "Wolves shall succeed for teachers, grievous wolves." The metaphor of "wolves" as clergymen is Milton's reference to the corruption of the Anglican as well as the Catholic church. Michael lists their many hypocritical practices. Priests and clergymen have held to traditions rather than the truths of the Scriptures; they have concerned themselves with their own positions and titles; they have used secular power under the guise of spiritual power to quiet dissenters; and the "Spirit of Grace itself" is bound by the observance of ritual in the church. These were all points that Milton had touched on in his earlier writings. The passage alludes to the condition of the Anglican church in the wake of the Protestant Reformation which had already become corrupt and ritualistic by the seventeenth century. When Milton writes about "secular power, though feigning still to act/ By spiritual," we are reminded of the political power of Archbishop Laud whose suppressive practices in the Anglican church were given complete support by Charles I.

Michael finishes his account of the "world restored" in which Christ will reward the faithful ones and create for them a new Heaven and Earth. In his enthusiasm about the news of salvation and the prospect of eternal happiness, Adam is suddenly overcome with joy when he sees that God is merciful.

> That all this good of evil shall produce,
> And evil turn to good; more wonderful
> Than that which by creation first brought forth
> Light out of darkness.

Adam feels that his fall has created an even better Paradise than the one that was lost. This is often referred to as the *felix culpa* or "fortunate fall," translated literally from the Latin as the "happy fault." It is a paradox that the fall is the worst human misfortune, but at the same time it is God's highest opportunity for good. God has chosen to turn evil into good. It is Adam's hope and sustains him as he prepares to face his ultimate expulsion from Paradise.

When Eve awakes from her restful sleep, she is prepared to leave with Adam. "With thee to go,/ Is to stay here; without thee here to stay,/ Is to go hence unwilling." These words echo those of Ruth in the Bible who says, "Whither thou goest, I will go; and where thou lodgest, I will lodge" (Ruth 1:16). Eve has made peace with her guilt. Though she is still aware that "all by me is lost," she also finds hope in the knowledge that "by me the Promised Seed shall all restore."

As Adam prepares to leave Paradise, we reflect on his development from his innocence before the fall, to his sin and consequent repentance and reconciliation with God, and finally to his realization that God is just and "to obey is best." This is the sum of all his wisdom. He now knows his place as Man in a world filled with woe, but he also has hope that Christ will restore that world. As Adam and Eve slowly find "their solitary way" on a foreign plain, their feelings of hope are mixed with sadness as they shed "some natural tears" over their loss of Paradise.

Study Questions

1. What approach does Michael use to explain how the world will be restored?

2. Which seventeenth-century monarch can be compared to the character of Nimrod from the Bible?

3. Besides an empire, what did Nimrod build?

4. Who is the first leader of the mighty nation of Israel?

5. Who is sent to deliver the nation of Israel out of captivity?

6. Who is the enemy of the Israelites?

7. What becomes of Solomon's people?

8. Who baptizes the first believers after Christ's death?

9. Where is Eve while Michael is talking to Adam?

10. Who accompanies Michael as he leads Adam and Eve out of Paradise?

Answers

1. Michael uses the method of narration to explain the restoration of a sinful world to Adam.

2. Most commentators feel that Milton was equating Charles I to Nimrod.

3. Nimrod built the Tower of Babel.

4. Abraham is the first leader of Israel.

5. Moses is sent to deliver the nation of Israel out of captivity.

6. Pharaoh and the Egyptians are the enemies of Moses and the Israelites.

7. Solomon's people are taken into captivity by the Babylonians.

8. The Apostles baptize the first believers after Christ's death.

9. Eve has been sleeping while Michael was speaking to Adam.

10. The Cherubim stand guard as God's brandished sword blazes in the sky in front of them.

Suggested Essay Topics

1. Adam feels that his fall has created an even better Paradise than the one that was lost. Explain the "fortunate fall." Is Adam's fall really fortunate? What price has been paid for this so-called "fortunate fall"? Explain your answer with examples from the poem.

2. Adam makes the statement that "to obey is best." Explicate this passage in the light of Adam's development. Why does Michael call this the sum of Adam's wisdom? Support your answer with examples from the epic.

Sample Analytical Paper Topics

The following paper topics are designed to test your understanding of the epic poem as a whole and to analyze important themes and literary devices. Following each question is a sample outline to help you get started.

Topic #1

Throughout the poem, Satan slowly degenerates from a fallen archangel, who still possesses some of the qualities of his former state in Heaven, to a completely depraved creature after the fall of Man. Write an essay tracing Satan's progressive degeneration that slowly conforms to the evil inside of him, illustrating the idea that spirit and matter are interconnected.

Outline

I.   Thesis Statement: *After his fall, Satan degenerates throughout the poem as he suffers the loss of his former luster, imbrutes himself in the body of a serpent, and finally undergoes a complete metamorphosis as a serpent in Hell.*

II. Satan degenerates from his former luster in Heaven.

   A. Pride brings him down

      1. Satan feels it is "better to reign in Hell than serve in Heaven."

2.   Satan denies that God created him.

3.   Allows no one to go to Earth with him because he wants the glory.

B.   Revenge against God

1.   He calls a council in Hell and then manipulates the vote.

2.   He decides to corrupt God's newest creation, Man.

C.   Ambivalence on Mount Niphates

1.   He refuses to repent, though he knows his rebellion against God is unwarranted.

2.   He decides to practice falsehood under saintly show.

III.   Satan degenerates by imbruting himself in the form of a serpent.

A.   Entering the serpent's body is an act of stealth.

1.   He searches for the serpent at midnight so he will not be caught.

2.   Darkness and evil surround the intended act against God and Man.

B.   Entering the serpent's body is humiliating.

1.   Satan resents the fact that he has descended to a beast.

2.   He lives for the glory he will receive from his fallen angels in Hell.

C.   Satan tempts Eve in the form of a serpent.

1.   He causes the fall of Man.

2.   After Eve's fall the Serpent slinks guiltily back into the thicket.

IV.   Satan's metamorphosis into a Serpent is complete degeneration.

A.   The Son curses the Serpent.

1.   He must grovel on his belly and stay in the form in which he sinned.

2. The Son prophesies that Christ will someday bruise the evil Serpent's heel and destroy Sin and Death.

B. God turns Satan's followers into a race of Serpent's.

V. Conclusion: Satan's steady degeneration has led him from a fallen angel whose "original brightness" is still apparent when he addresses his legions in Hell, to a completely depraved creature who is metamorphosed into a Serpent.

Topic #2

Milton's consciousness of the natural order is based on the hierarchy in the scale of Nature. This hierarchy must never be broken, the lower usurping the position of the higher, or the result will be disastrous. Write an essay analyzing this seventeenth-century idea in relation to some of the major characters in *Paradise Lost*.

Outline

I. Thesis Statement: *The hierarchy in the scale of Nature has been broken by Satan, Adam, and Eve in* Paradise Lost *which has led to disorder and chaos in an otherwise orderly world.*

II. Satan has attempted to usurp God's power.

A. Satan rebels against God in Heaven.

1. He denies that God created him and begins the war in Heaven.

2. He and his followers are driven out of Heaven and into Hell.

B. Satan brings sin into the world.

1. He beguiles Eve to disobey God, convincing her to eat the forbidden fruit.

2. He mocks God when he returns to Hell.

III. Eve has exalted herself above her natural place.

A. Eve suggests that she and Adam divide their labors.

1. Eve enters into a debate with Adam, presenting her own point of view.

2. Eve is hurt by Adam's inability to trust her alone.

B. Eve decides to go against Adam's better judgment.

C. Eve disobeys God's command.

   1. Eve allows her reason to be swayed by her passion when she tastes the forbidden fruit.

   2. The Serpent flatters Eve, telling her lies against God that she believes.

D. Eve considers withholding her God-like knowledge from Adam in order to "render her more equal" or even superior to Adam.

IV. Adam has allowed himself to be held in subjection to Eve.

A. Adam's passion for Eve sways his judgment.

   1. Adam perceives her as the wisest and best of creation.

   2. Raphael forewarns Adam about exalting Eve above her natural place.

B. Adam allows Eve to go out alone in spite of his fears for her safety.

C. Adam accepts the forbidden fruit from Eve.

   1. He cannot face living alone in the forest again without Eve.

   2. The Son rebukes Adam for letting Eve act as his God.

V. Conclusion: In a world where Satan claims equality with God; Eve boldly chooses to work separately from Adam; and Adam cannot face living without Eve, disaster is a natural result because the hierarchy of Nature has been broken.

Topic #3

Throughout his development, Adam has evolved from a happy stage of innocence before the fall to an acceptance of God's justice in a sinful world. Write an essay tracing Adam's process of development as he learns to reconcile himself with his mortal existence after the fall.

Outline

I. Thesis Statement: *Adam evolves from a stage of innocence before the fall to his sin and consequent repentance and reconciliation with God, and finally to his acceptance of God's justice in an imperfect world.*

II. Adam is innocent in the beginning of *Paradise Lost.*

   A. He is devoted to God.

      1. He offers prayers of praise and adoration morning and evening.

      2. He obeys God's commands.

   B. He possesses an inordinate passion for Eve.

      1. Adam becomes weak in her presence.

      2. Eve seems the most wise and virtuous being in Paradise.

III. Adam then moves into a sinful stage.

   A. Adam experiences a period of despair and hopelessness.

      1. He first mourns the loss of his idyllic Paradise.

      2. He then blames Eve for leading him into sin.

   B. Adam reconciles with Eve.

      1. Eve takes all the blame.

      2. Adam forgives Eve, suggesting they stop blaming each other.

IV. Adam repents and reconciles with God.

   A. Adam decides that he wants to live and propagate the race.

      1. The Serpent's head will be bruised by his offspring as God had promised.

      2. They will avenge Satan's sinful deed.

   B. Adam falls prostrate before God, asking his forgiveness.

      1. Adam is told by Michael that God has heard their prayers and forgiven them.

        2.   Michael tells them that they must leave the garden.

V.   Adam accepts God's justice in a sinful world.

    A.   Visions of the future help Adam continue living.

        1.   Adam gains a perspective on the consequences of his fall.

        2.   The meaning of Death is clarified by examples of Death and war.

    B.   Michael narrates the story of Christ's death, resurrection, and ascension.

        1.   Adam now understands how Christ's resurrection will crush the Serpent's head by destroying Sin and Death.

        2.   Adam understands his part in the lineage of Christ.

VI.   Conclusion: Adam evolves from innocence to sin and repentance. Eve's selfless concern while he is in the depths of despair, and Michael's subsequent education of Adam are an integral part of the process that leads him to an acceptance of the justice of God by the end of the epic.

SECTION FOUR

Bibliography

Primary Source

Milton, John. *The Poems of John Milton*, ed. James Holly Hanford. New York: The Ronald Press Company, 1953.

Secondary Sources

Aristotle. *The Politics*, ed. Trevor J. Saunders. London: Penguin Books Ltd., 1992.

Gardner, Helen. *A Reading of Paradise Lost*. London: Oxford University Press,1965.

Holy Bible, King James Version. New York: Collins' Clear-type Press, 1956.

Hamilton, Edith. *Mythology*. New York: The New American Library, 1942.

Lewis, C. S. *A Preface to Paradise Lost*. New York: Oxford University Press, 1961.

Milton Modern Essays in Criticism, ed. Arthur E. Barker. New York: Oxford University Press, 1965.

Milton Paradise Lost, ed. A. E. Dyson and Julian Lovelock. London: Macmillan Press Ltd., 1973.

On Milton's Poetry, ed. Arnold Stein. New York: Fawcett Publications, Inc., 1970.

Rajan, B. *Paradise Lost and the Seventeenth Century Reader*. New York: Oxford University Press, 1948.

Shakespeare, William. *The Riverside Shakespeare*, ed. G. Blakemore Evans. Boston: Houghton Mifflin Company, 1974.

Sims, James H. *The Bible in Milton's Epics.* Gainesville: University of Florida Press, 1962.

Spenser, Edmund. *Selected Poetry*, ed. Leo Kirschbaum. New York: Holt, Rinehart and Winston, 1965.

Vergil. *The Aeneid*, ed. Moses Hadas. London: Bantam Books, Inc., 1965.

West, Robert H. *Milton and the Angels.* Athens: University of Georgia Press, 1955.

Introducing...

MAXnotes

REA's Literature Study Guides

MAXnotes™ offer a fresh look at masterpieces of literature, presented in a lively and interesting fashion. **MAXnotes**™ offer the essentials of what you should know about the work, including outlines, explanations and discussions of the plot, character lists, analyses, and historical context. **MAXnotes**™ are designed to help you think independently about literary works by raising various issues and thought-provoking ideas and questions. Written by literary experts who currently teach the subject, **MAXnotes**™ enhance your understanding and enjoyment of the work.

Available **MAXnotes**™ include the following:

Animal Farm	The Great Gatsby	Moby-Dick
Beowulf	Hamlet	1984
Brave New World	Huckleberry Finn	Of Mice and Men
The Canterbury Tales	I Know Why the	The Odyssey
The Catcher in the Rye	Caged Bird Sings	Paradise Lost
The Crucible	The Iliad	Plato's Republic
Death of a Salesman	Julius Caesar	A Raisin in the Sun
Divine Comedy I-Inferno	King Lear	Romeo and Juliet
Gone with the Wind	Les Misérables	The Scarlet Letter
The Grapes of Wrath	Lord of the Flies	A Tale of Two Cities
Great Expectations	Macbeth	To Kill a Mockingbird

RESEARCH & EDUCATION ASSOCIATION
61 Ethel Road W. • Piscataway, New Jersey 08854
Phone: (908) 819-8880

Please send me more information about MAXnotes™.

Name _____

Address _____

City _____ State _____ Zip _____